All brand names and product names used in this book are trademarks or registered trademarks of their respective owners. The use of these names is for identification purposes only and does not imply endorsement.

This is a work of nonfiction. The views expressed are those of the author. Every effort has been made to ensure accuracy at the time of publication. This book is not intended as legal, financial, or professional advice. Any resemblance to actual persons is coincidental and unintentional.

No part of this publication may be reproduced, stored in a retrieval system, or transmitted in any form or by any means—electronic, mechanical, photocopying, recording, or otherwise—without prior written permission of the publisher, except in the case of brief quotations in critical articles or reviews.

ISBN (paperback):
ISBN (ebook):

Printed in the United States of America

10 9 8 7 6 5 4 3 2 1

First edition

Published by Jersey City Press

Cover and interior design by Andrew Lawrence
Edited by Jeff Gelberg

Copyright © 2026 by John Long
All rights reserved.

ZOMBIE BRANDS

How brands lost their humanity—and how they can regain their appeal in the age of AI.

by
John Long

For my Father

A "Mad Men" era media guy who had a
head for numbers and the soul of
a creative.

Table of Contents

How it started / how it's going.

In May, 2021, I noticed a banner ad—don't remember on which website—for a well-known vodka brand. Even allowing for the fact banner ads have set an appallingly low bar when it comes to creative quality, this particular one was Hall-of-Fame level awful. The headline, "Delicious drinks, Memorable moments" actually made me laugh out loud. The image couldn't possibly have been more pedestrian: a bottle (completely full), next to a glass (completely full), on a table (set and completely untouched), with some blurred-out people clumsily staged in the background (no talent fee!). But the "chef's kiss" element was a large, white, oversized button with those two immortal, all-powerful words no Internet user can possibly resist: "LEARN MORE." It was as though whoever or whatever actually made this monstrosity had been tasked with distilling all of the worst trends in digital advertising into a single ad—and succeeded brilliantly.

As I marveled in the banner's majestic banality, something started to bother me. I noticed the name at the top of the ad, above that ridiculous headline. Even though here it was marred by an unnecessary period mark and a distracting (R) symbol, it was nevertheless once a proud brand name that used to mean something—especially in the advertising industry. It bestrode this sad collection of pixels defiantly: **ABSOLUT**.

Then I got angry. Because when my eyes dropped down on the bottle again, I was reminded of one of the most iconic advertising campaigns of the past half century—"Absolut Perfection" by TBWA. It ran for 25 years, transforming an obscure Swedish vodka brand into a global spirits giant and cultural icon. The campaign was so wildly popular, people who'd never even had a sip of Absolut—let alone bought a bottle—tore the ads out of magazines. The ads papered the walls of millions of college dorms and adorned t-shirts. (Side question: ever see a banner ad on a t-shirt?)

What a disgrace, I thought, to treat a brand that had done so much good work for so long—and owed so much to great craft—so carelessly. Then, because I was pretty deep into Twitter memes at the time, I posted these two images under "How it started/how it's going":

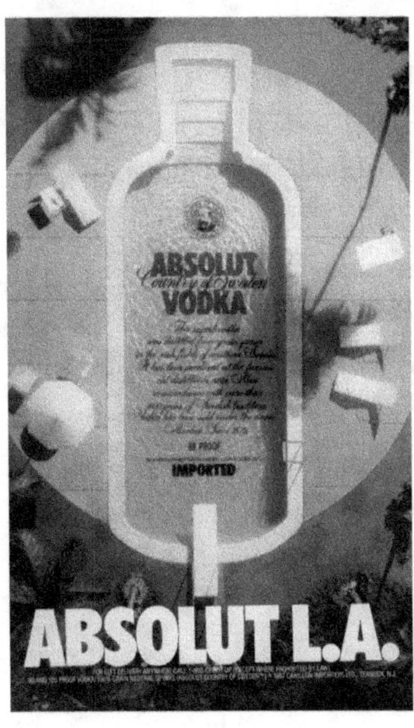

I'd actually done a similar juxtaposition two years earlier, with a Rolex print ad and banner ad. But this time, probably because I framed it in a meme—and because that classic Absolut campaign was so beloved—it got a decent amount of likes and comments. And I realized I'd hit on something.

So over the course of the next year, every few weeks, I added another to the series. No brand was spared. If I spotted a crappy social post or shabby banner ad in the wild from a brand that had traditionally done great work, they got called out. The list got very long: Porsche, Nikon, Mini Cooper, Levis, Volvo, Land Rover, Mercedes, American Express, Harley Davidson, BMW, Louis Vuitton, Chivas Regal, Perrier—even Apple. All of them deservedly got the "How it started / how it's going" treatment.

One day, after spotting another one of my "How it started / how it's going" posts, one of my advertising Twitter pals suggested I create a master thread of the entire series. I was a little embarrassed I hadn't thought of that myself, so I obliged. I couldn't believe what happened next: it went viral. That term is badly overused, but in this case, it's true. The compiled thread shot up quickly and racked up over 1M views, was shared all over the world, and was written about in a UK-based publication that covers the ad industry. The juxtaposition of ambitious, intelligent, well-crafted communication with the pathetic, dreary emptiness of the banner ads—both from the same brand—struck a nerve.

That viral Twitter thread inspired *Zombie Brands*. It's my attempt to explain how brands "started" by trying to be as attractive as possible to as many people as possible, gradually abandoned that basic approach, and became what I call Zombie Brands—soulless, unfeeling, inarticulate goons that maniacally target and harass people in the pursuit of what sustains them: clicks.

Zombie Brands is not an argument that "everything was better" during the "Mad Men" era, that no terrible ads were produced before the Internet, or that brands today should go back to investing heavily in print advertising.

But it does attempt to make the case that, due to several business and cultural trends, the current course of bombarding people with cheap, unappealing, and undifferentiated messages is both unsustainable and damaging to the long-term health of brands. And it offers what I believe are useful suggestions on how brands can regain their allure. But first, let's talk about what a Zombie Brand is and how they came to be.

Invasion of the Zombie Brands.

Imagine you have a neighbor named Brad. Brad's a used car salesman and kind of a schlub. He never deviates from his almost comically-stereotypical wardrobe for a suburban, middle-aged salesman: pleated khakis, plain golf shirt, brown loafers with those fussy little tassels.

Oh, and he's also a total bore. The thing about Brad is, every time you run into him—which always seems to be at the worst possible time—he can't stop talking about himself. He drones on and on about what he's doing at work, how good his deals are, how his golf game is going, his promotion. He never bothers to ask how you are or make pleasant small talk other to blurt out "Happy Independence Day!" or "Happy President's Day!" or "Happy National Roadtrip Day!"

The worst part? He never stops trying to sell you a car. You get texts and emails from him like this every single week, without fail.

"Hey, neighbor! You've got to come on down to the lot and check out these deals we've got!"

"John! Ready for a new ride? Just got an SUV you'll love."

"Hi, John! That sedan your driving's getting a bit long in the tooth. When are we going to talk trade in?!"

You'd absolutely hate that guy, wouldn't you? Well, sadly, the way Brad acts is exactly the way too many brands are showing up in the marketplace today. They're drab, boring, look and sound like everyone else, constantly talk about themselves— and never stop shoving offers in your face. Annoying.

But back to Brad. One Saturday morning, while you're picking up your newspaper in your driveway, he's trying sell you a Mustang. All of a sudden he begins repeating your name over and over, faster and faster, then suddenly lurches forward, falls down, and cracks his head open—revealing he was a robot all along.

Creepy, right? Well, turns out a lot of what brands do today is driven by automation and digital technology (when was the last time you reached an actual person on a company's help line?). They're not only dull, impersonal and annoying, they're often not even *human.*

That's a Zombie Brand: a soulless, unfeeling, uncaring, used car-selling automaton. And an unfortunate number of companies have decided to turn most of their marketing budgets over these monsters.

What the Rose Bowl game and engagement rings have in common.

Stop for a second and ask yourself these two questions:

1. How many ads in the past year have made you
   laugh, cry, or feel any emotion at all?
2. How many ads from the past year can you recall?

I'm guessing you're not able to recall more than a handful—if that. And that's a serious long-term business problem for brands. As John Hegarty, one of the founder of BBH said,

"A brand is the most valuable piece of real estate in the world; a corner of someone's mind."

There's a story that illustrates this idea nicely. A 42-year old man sells his start-up company at a huge profit. He's suddenly very wealthy, and a friend asks him what he's going to do with all that money.

"The very first thing I'm going to do," the man answers, "is buy a Porsche."

"Why?" the friend asks.

"I saw an ad for a 911," says the man, "when I was 12."

Now that's a good, albeit extreme example, of how advertising used to work. Being attractive, creating desire, and doing so in a way that was extremely memorable. Creating immediate demand and building long-term value was the goal. But the reason you, dear reader, can't recall more than a couple of ads you've seen this year—let alone three decades later like the man in that story—is because brands today have largely given up on building long-term value, instead opting to bombard you with the digital equivalent of windshield fliers, hoping through sheer incessant, mechanical pestering you'll keep them top of mind.

This is a recent development. For most of the past hundred years, brands tried very hard to make themselves—above all—appealing. Brands wanted as many people as possible to *like* them. And not just their customers. They spent an enormous amount of resources winning hearts and minds, even ones that weren't necessarily buying what they were selling at that particular moment.

Brands tried to appeal to people through a wide variety of mediums, forms, and techniques advertising agencies had developed over many decades to make them irresistible. Vibrant colors. Distinctive typefaces. Memorable taglines ("A diamond is forever," "Reach out and touch someone," "Have a Coke and a smile," "Just do it", "Think different", "I'm lovin' it,"). Jingles. Mascots. Extravaganzas. Contests. Celebrity endorsements. Just to name a few. They created entirely new forms of entertainment for the twin giants of twentieth century media—radio and television—and through their patronage (ie., media spend)—brought them into your home, completely free of charge.

It's fashionable today for advertising professionals to opine about how brands should "participate in culture." Brands used to create culture. Soap operas? Thanks, Proctor & Gamble. A parade on Thanksgiving? Thanks, Gimbel's and Macy's. The Rose Bowl game? Thanks, Pasadena Valley Hunt Club. Diamonds as the standard engagement ring gemstone? Thanks, DeBeers (and of course their agency, the advertising behemoth of the first half of the twentieth century, N.W. Ayer—which also invented that 'engagement ring should cost three months salary' rule through, you guessed it, an advertising campaign).

This myriad of efforts to attract new converts worked remarkably well, and made names like Marlboro, McDonald's and Maybelline famous all over the world. What's been forgotten is that success wasn't due solely to the fact mass media had such an enormous reach. It was also because people like brands for the same exact reasons they like people.

Back to Brad. Let's flip our thought experiment around and consider what a Bizarro Brad would look like, sound like, and act. For one, he's a sharp dresser—always looks put together. He's also an excellent conversationalist in the sense he talks about things you didn't know but you find interesting, and seems to share your interests. He has a distinctive voice with a slight regional accent to go with a memorable delivery. He's a good listener, and understands where you're coming from. He doesn't pester you. He can be quite funny. He always seems to show up at just the right time when you need him, as if by magic. He makes you think. Every so often, you even learn something from him. And above all, he isn't constantly hitting you up for money and trying to sell you something. But on the occasions he does—and he most definitely sells—he's charming and persuasive.

In my view, Bizarro Brad is how the most successful brands tried to behave as a matter of course. They may not have succeeded at all of those things, but directionally, it's broadly what they were attempting to do.

From persuasion to pestering.

So what happened? How did brands morph from the kind of people you wanted to hang out with into zombies? I believe four really big developments over the past three decades explains this radical shift: the Internet, digital media, social media, and smartphones.

The Internet broke mass media. It disrupted print, radio, and television, the channels brands used so successfully to reach mass audiences for decades. It destroyed magazines, decimated newspapers, and enabled the streaming service ecosystem in which people can completely avoid audio or filmed advertising for a price. That in turn meant there was no longer a broadly-shared mass culture. It also made the transmission of digital media possible.

Digital media and non-linear editing made it incredibly cheap and easy to produce still and moving images, which had the effect of reducing craft. Stock photography and music libraries—which could be easily accessed and re-shared digitally—made original photography shoots and musical scores seem like unnecessary luxuries to brands eager to slash marketing budgets. With digital media, they could not only save on production, they could also scrimp on distribution (media spend) with social media.

Social media gave brands direct access to millions of people. It also tricked them into thinking people wanted to engage with them in the same way they did with their friends and family. Because social media channels weren't originally designed to be supported by ads, they've all had the same problem trying to figure out, after the fact, how to jam ads into their endless scrolls. Social media's meteoric rise was turbocharged by a piece of hardware called the smartphone.

Smartphones, those highly-addictive, likely harmful personal computers we all have attached to our bodies at any given time occupy an oversized chunk of our attention, which robs it from other media. Smartphones' small screens make it difficult to tell rich, impactful brand stories, and the apps that run on these devices make it possible for users to avoid them all together.

It's important to note here I'm not some Luddite, or even a technology skeptic. I'll bet I've been online longer than just about anyone you know—since 1984—a full decade before most people had even heard of the "World Wide Web." That's the year I got my first 300-baud, dial-up modem and a CompuServe account for my Apple IIe. I've been a creative director at three of the most successful digital agencies in the world—Huge, Code & Theory, and now Digitas. And I'm not one to romanticize the advertising industry of the past. Although I'm a second-generation ad guy—my father worked on Madison Avenue during the Mad Men era—I'm well aware there was no shortage of terrible ads in years past, and I remember plenty of them. (Google "Calgon" and "Ancient Chinese Secret"—that monstrosity still haunts me.)

There's no question all four of these technologies not only

chipped away at brands' images, degrading how they showed up in the marketplace—they fundamentally shifted their overall marketing philosophy away from mass appeal to *targeting*. Instead of aiming for fame and persuasion—they bombarded a narrowly-defined customer with incessant demands to BUY NOW. Instead of carefully creating stuff people wanted to read or watch or experience, they opted instead for mercilessly pounding them into submission with an endless avalanche of spam.

You might argue brands have always used a portion of their marketing budgets for direct, one-to-one activities to drive sales. And that's true. But most used direct marketing as a compliment to their mass advertising—not to the exclusion of it.

Besides, I'm talking less about actual budgets and more about an overall philosophy. It's simply the case that brands today care much less about being appealing as much as using data to identify and bombard key prospects and current customers.

On the surface, there's a kind of logic to this. Why waste all that time and money talking to people who aren't in the market? Isn't it much more *efficient* to target only people who are likely to buy—especially if data allows you to identify them? Why blow all those dollars on people who aren't going to buy what you're selling? That very well may be in the short term. But fame for fame's sake is in brands' long-term interest. Back to Hegarty:

"One of the most profound and fundamental things you can say about the value of a brand is that it is made by people who will never buy it."

Indeed. The problem with exclusively talking to who you think are your customers *right now* is you're excluding people who might be your customers in six months, a year, or five years from now. So while it may be more efficient to target them in the short term, there's an opportunity cost over the long term. You're essentially robbing future Peter to pay present Paul.

Here's a simple example. I will never buy a Patek Phillipe wristwatch. I love my Omega Speedmaster, and Patek just isn't my style. But Patek also happens to be an insanely expensive brand, even among luxury timepieces. The Nautilus, one of Patek's most coveted models, will set you back a cool $170,000. So yeah, not for me. And yet, I know all about Patek. I know about their Swiss heritage. I've seen their advertising, which is quite good for the category. Since 1996, they've been running a campaign featuring black and white photography of wealthy-looking fathers and their young sons, wearing expensive clothes and doing expensive things, anchored by the tagline, "You never actually own a Patek Phillipe. You merely look after it for the next generation." That's not only a great line, it's an extraordinarily artful rationalization for dropping $170K on a watch. "Don't feel guilty, you're not buying it for yourself, you're buying it for your son!" Genius. So because of all of this, I recognize a Patek every time I see one in movies or television—which is frequent, and definitely not a coincidence.

Having said all that, ask yourself: do you think Patek would be able to charge $170,000 for a watch if it had only targeted the microscopically-tiny subset of the population that can afford a Patek? Of course not.

The fact is, as much as technology has changed, human beings haven't. For all the talk about how tech has "re-wired" our brains, we still don't like people like our friend Brad—let alone the Zombie Brand version of him. I'm convinced that, if brands keep behaving like zombies, they're going to eventually lose customers, because the generation that was born in the first two decades of this century mostly only know brands' zombie selves. And they are not going to be loyal to them as they age.

How do I know? The answer is wrapped up in the concept of "brand" itself. There are a lot of definitions of that word, but I'm particularly fond of this one, from the former CEO of Disney, Michael Eisner.

"A brand is a living entity, and it is enriched or undermined cumulatively over time, the product of a thousand small gestures."

Another way of saying that is a brand is the sum total of your impressions of a company or product. That actually has huge implications. It means *everything* a brand says and does impacts the brand whether it's a logo, typeface, product, a radio spot, packaging, employees' uniforms, event, the cleanliness of a store, tagline, the "on hold" music, coupon, an email—and yes, even a banner ad. All those impressions add up over time, which is why brands used to be extremely picky about what they put their logo on. The strongest brands were fanatical about this. They understood the more crappy experiences you have with a brand, the less likely you are to keeping giving it your business. At some point, those crappy experiences reach a tipping point in your mind and you won't give the brand another cent.

Here's the weird part. I don't know anyone, I mean anyone in the advertising industry that disagrees with that basic formulation of brand, and those subsequent implications. Yet we've all been sort of pretending over the past decade or so that spam emails, lousy banners and automated call centers won't over time have a deleterious effect on a brand. Sorry people, we're kidding ourselves. Everything contributes to the brand. Everything matters.

In the next few chapters, I'm going to demonstrate specifically how those four technologies—the Internet, digital media, smartphones and social media—turned brands into zombies. In the book's second half, I'll offer some ways for brands to get their mojo back, using the very tools that undermined them in the first place.

Zombie Brands all look alike.

2

It's not hard to make the case that how a brand looks is important. The term "brand" itself comes from the practice of branding livestock, which dates all the way back to the ancient Egyptians. A livestock brand, above all, has to be distinctive and recognizable enough to identify the branded animal's owner. Fun fact: today, many states still regulate livestock brands through livestock agencies, and in Arizona, it's actually illegal for two ranchers to own the same brand.

Branding on products, the kind of brand we mostly think of today, took off in the nineteenth century, when industrialization enabled companies to produce, ship and sell packaged goods all across the country. That was a huge shift because before then, when you needed, say, flour, you'd go to your local general store—there was probably only one in town—and buy the generic flour that came in a sack labeled "FLOUR." And that flour was almost certainly produced in a local or regional mill, and sold directly to the general store.

But with the advent of mass production and railroads, companies could churn out thousands of tons of flour, and instead of just selling to one town or region, they could ship it all over the country. Suddenly, that plain sack needed a label to distinguish it from its competitors. Like this one:

(Founded in 1869, Minneapolis, Minnesota-based Pillsbury went on to become the largest flour producer in the United States by the 1890s. The power of branding!)

So above all, the central obligation of a brand has always been visual differentiation. It's kind of the whole point of brand. Which is one of the strangest aspects of Zombie Brands— they forgot this fundamental rule. Let's start with a brand's most important asset: its logo.

First, they came for the logos.

The oldest, continually-used logo in the world dates to the fourteenth century and belongs to Stella Artois, which has been using the same horn icon since 1366. In 1717, they added a star.

Although most companies don't maintain their logos nearly as long as Stella, they're usually pretty reluctant to alter them. For one, there's always the danger a new logo will irritate or confuse customers—and that will have a harmful effect on loyalty or new sales. People generally don't like change, especially when it's something they like or are accustomed to. If you happen to follow the advertising trade press, you've probably noticed at least two or three major brands trot out a new logo every year, only to be greeted with Bronx cheers. (I think companies unveiling their new logos with splashy press releases is a questionable practice in itself, but I digress.)

Another reason companies prefer not to alter their logos is that it's time-consuming and expensive. The bigger the company, the harder and more expensive it is to modify it. As someone who has been a part of several rebrands, including at *The Economist,* believe me—it's a massive undertaking.

Finally, companies maintain their logos' status quo because their very identity is intertwined with them—it's who *they are.* Now, when companies do change who they are—in the form of radical structural changes or new leadership—logos often reflect that as if to signal to the marketplace, "there's something new happening here." To cite one example, one of the first things Steve Jobs did when he returned to Apple in 1997 was to rebrand the company from its iconic "rainbow" apple icon to a much more restrained, all-black version. Its minimalist aesthetic signaled a new era for the company, a sensibility it broadly maintains today.

But almost all the incentives are aligned against a company messing with its logo. There are dozens more reasons not to do it than to do it. That's why the trend over the past decade or so has been so jarring to people who follow this stuff. It's not just that brands have been much more willing to futz with their logos—some of which were among the most storied and prestigious in the world. It's that they've been stripping away the elements that make those logos unique.

Here are five notable examples.

YVES SAINT LAURENT $\longrightarrow$ **SAINT LAURENT**

BALENCIAGA $\longrightarrow$ **BALENCIAGA**

BURBERRY
London, England $\longrightarrow$ **BURBERRY**
LONDON ENGLAND

Berluti
Paris $\longrightarrow$ **BERLUTI**
PARIS

BALMAIN
PARIS $\longrightarrow$ **BALMAIN**
PARIS

Smartphones, dumb logos.

The trend toward simplification is clear. Logos were being over-simplified to the point of rendering them essentially generic. They're turning into your neighbor Brad, wearing the same khakis and golf shirts and loafers as everyone else.

So why did this happen? Maybe the minimalist aesthetic tech brands like Apple and then Google adopted had grown more and more popular in the subsequent decades, and just taken over everything. Or perhaps today's CMOs, under pressure from CEOs and boards of directors and pressed for time (average tenure in 2025: under four years) want to make their mark—so they have an incentive to rebrand the organization. But I think the actual culprit is pixels.

Smartphones play such an outsized role in the current digital media ecosystem that companies spend a lot of time obsessing about how they look on them. Now, it follows that if you prioritize optimizing your logo for tiny screens and social icons—if that's literally the most important thing to you— you're probably going to have to simplify your logo, perhaps radically. The problem with whittling logos down to the point they "work" perfectly on smartphones is that process often erases what makes them distinctive in the first place.

This isn't just an aesthetic problem. It's a business problem. Remember, the whole point of a brand is to look different. So if brands start to blend together, will it hurt them?

In 2023, Distinctive BAT (distinctivebat.com), a UK-based brand consultancy, set out to answer that question. They tested the "before and after" logos of 16 famous brands that had recently been redesigned. What they found was the process of whittling down brands—for the most part—actually increased the likelihood of misattribution.

BAT Distinctiveness Score

Asset Recognition + Brand Attribution – Misattribution

How to read: A max score of 200 means 100% of people recognise the debranded asset, 100% of people attribute it to the correct brand, and 0 people misattribute it to another category brand.

Brand	Score (Old)	Uplifts	Score (New)
Sprite	59	35	24
Warner Bros	117	77	40
Post It	50	6	56
Peugeot	134	80	54
Pfizer	43	21	22
Durex	73	49	24
Rolling Stone	15	21	-6
Toyota	140	3	143
Subway	160	38	122
Burberry	29	14	15
Pringles	153	18	135
Toblerone	126	62	64
Intel	68	92	-24
Burger King	141	1	142
Volkswagen	181	10	171
Yves St Laurent	8	1	7

Nationally representative sample of 750 U.K. consumers, Jan 2023

They concluded:

The oversimplification of logos (and brand worlds) has several downsides. The first and most obvious is that any logo change disrupts memory structures and diminishes its use as a branding device. The breadth of this diminishment is really down to how far the logo strays from its original guise or, in extreme cases, how legible it is...In the short term, this would have an impact on brand attribution for any advertising, reducing the impact in terms of salience and advertising message association.

It's certainly not always the case that "simpler" means "worse." The Distinctive BAT study showed that Burger King managed to simplify to its advantage, and I'd cite my former client, Starbucks, as another example of that.

In this case, Starbucks was so globally famous by 2011 when they rebranded that most people recognized their distinct green mermaid—so losing the brand name didn't hurt them. And because Starbucks sells a lot more than just coffee, removing that word actually better represented what the company offers.

But it's clear that in their quest for smartphone optimization, too many brands sacrificed too much of their logos' distinctiveness.

There's nothing funny about Comic Sans.

After logos, typefaces are one of a brand's foundational elements. I'm a writer by trade but a bit of a typeface nerd. Maybe it's because I believe in the importance of words, it follows I would care about how they look. It's also undoubtedly the case that a typeface, when chosen carefully and used consistently, can help define a brand. Here are two examples.

Sorry, no beige.

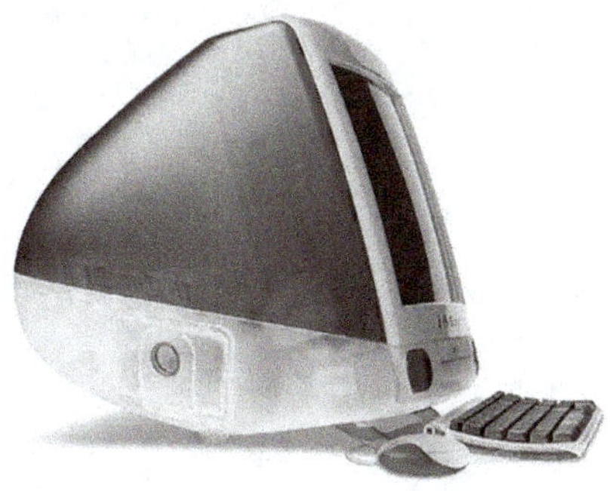

There's a strategy behind the typefaces these companies chose to represent their brand. Nike's choice of Futura Bold matched its bold, uncompromising tone of voice. Apple's preferred font for many years—a customized Garamond—was perhaps selected to amplify the company's meticulous product design and its association with creativity. (It's not surprising Steve Jobs, who studied calligraphy at Reed College, understood the importance of typefaces.)

Remember, back then, a decent chunk of a company's annual marketing budget was still going to print and out of home advertising, making these choices even more consequential. In print, companies could choose from literally thousands of typefaces, and customize them as they saw fit, in order to best reflect their brands. That all changed with the Internet.

Online, the wide variety of fonts a brand could select from suddenly shrank dramatically. Microsoft's 1996 Core fonts for the Web project, an attempt to standardize fonts for the Internet, featured just 11 fonts, which any user of a computer since that year will instantly recognize:

Andale Mono
Arial
Arial Black
Comic Sans
Courier
New Georgia
Impact
Times New Roman
Trebuchet MS
Verdana
Webdings

(The fact that Microsoft unleashed the scourge of Comic Sans on the world is one of the worst corporate crimes in human history.)

So as the "World Wide Web" quickly became the place brands published most of their content, they had to ditch the typeface they'd used in print and adopt some form of one of these. What's more, perhaps in service of brand consistency, brands started adopting these fonts across the board, into non-digital media. One of the most controversial examples of this involves a little Swedish home furnishings company called IKEA.

Paul Renner turns over in his grave.

IKEA is known all over the world for making excellence in design affordable. It's core to who they are. Since their founding, they had used a font called Futura in their advertising and communications, and most prominently in the catalog. What's so special about Futura? Well, Futura has a distinguished history, having been designed by the great typographer Paul Renner during the Bauhaus era, and is widely admired by designers to this day.

But in 2009, IKEA made the shocking decision to replace Futura with Verdana—not just on digital channels, but everywhere, including the catalog.

It was a baffling move that sparked outrage—and justifiably so. What does it say when a company which built its reputation on impeccable design chooses *Microsoft* over Paul Freaking Renner? Nothing good, I'd say. (Realizing their mistake, IKEA wisely reversed themselves in 2019.)

Even as web-friendly fonts have grown substantially since 1996, some variation of these core fonts—especially the san serifs—are still ubiquitous. When smartphones and their small screens became the medium brands started prioritizing, the range of choices narrowed even further.

Schlock photography.

After logos and typefaces, another visual element that can help set a brand apart in peoples' minds is photography. It's never been easy to develop an "ownable" house photography style and to execute it consistently, over a long period of time. And to be fair, very few brands have done so. Nike is one that comes to mind.

What makes these images great, aside from their artistic craft, is that there's real drama in them. The product isn't featured, because Nike isn't selling athletic gear, they're selling an ethos. They're selling "Just do it."

Dove is another brand that has done a consistently excellent job with making photography an integral part of their brand, going on two decades with the "Real Beauty" campaign.

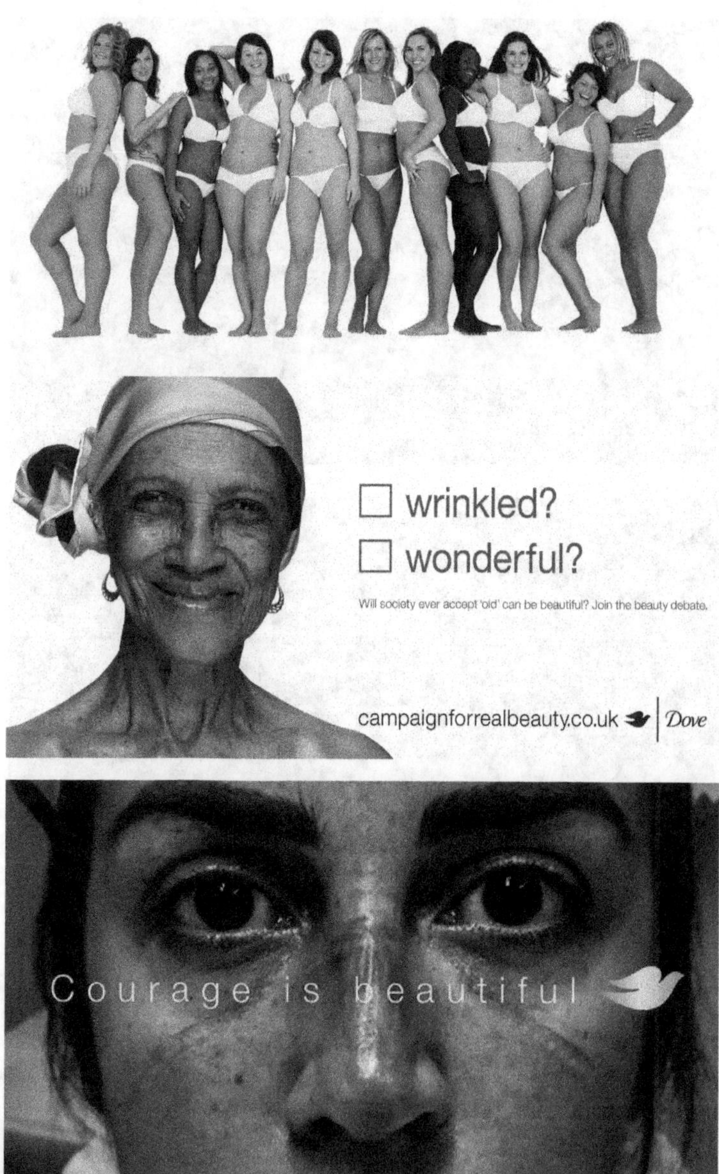

Now it's certainly true Nike has the advantage of being a category that's naturally teeming with drama—sports. It's also the case Dove made the strategic decision to stop focusing on product (good call—people know what soap is) and have the brand stand for a bigger idea—which opened up the possibility for beautiful, striking photography.

But what if you're selling, say, men's shirts? How do you make that interesting? How do you build a brand around shirts? Well, David Ogilvy had a solution for that back in the 1950s.

The man in the Hathaway shirt

AMERICAN MEN are beginning to realize that it is ridiculous to buy good suits and then spoil the effect by wearing an ordinary, mass-produced shirt. Hence the growing popularity of HATHAWAY shirts, which are in a class by themselves.

HATHAWAY shirts wear infinitely longer—a matter of years. They make you look younger and more distinguished, because of the subtle way HATHAWAY cut collars. The whole shirt is tailored more generously, and is therefore more comfortable. The tails are longer, and stay in your trousers. The buttons are mother-of-pearl. Even the stitching has an ante-bellum elegance about it.

Above all, HATHAWAY make their shirts of remarkable fabrics, collected from the four corners of the earth—Viyella, and Aertex, from England, woolen taffeta from Scotland, Sea Island cotton from the West Indies, hand-woven madras from India, broadcloth from Manchester, linen batiste from Paris, hand-blocked silks from England, exclusive cottons from the best weavers in America. You will get a great deal of quiet satisfaction out of wearing shirts which are in such impeccable taste.

HATHAWAY shirts are made by a small company of dedicated craftsmen in the little town of Waterville, Maine. They have been at it, man and boy, for one hundred and twenty years.

At better stores everywhere, or write C. F. HATHAWAY, Waterville, Maine, for the name of your nearest store. In New York, telephone OX 7-5566. Prices from $5.95 to $20.00.

Ogilvy's theory was that for a photo to be effective in advertising, it had to have what he called "story quality"—something in the image that made the viewer wonder: what's going on there? Who is that guy wearing the Hathaway shirt and why is he wearing an eye patch? There had to be just enough mystery in the photograph that you were compelled to read the copy. No one would've noticed that Man in the Hathaway Shirt without that eyepatch.

Stock photographs generally don't have a "story quality" because they aren't produced with an idea in mind—such as never giving up even if you're losing, or feeling comfortable in your own skin, or—that if that shirt is good enough for that proud gentleman who looks like he might be a veteran of the Battle of Ardennes, it's good enough for you. That means stock photos are inherently less useful in building a brand. What's more, stock photographs at their worst tend to reflect an almost theater-of-the-absurd phoniness—fake situations, fake smiles, badly-staged poses. People absolutely thrilled to be doing their taxes on their laptop. People downright giddy to be talking to their doctors. People super excited to be waxing their cars. There's a manic creepiness to photos like those. Can we ever get enough of two businessmen in suits shaking hands? Yes, yes we can.

In 2011, a blog called The Hairpin compiled a certain genre of stock photograph, and inspired an Internet meme: "Women Laughing Alone With Salad."

Because there's one thing that makes the ladies really crack up and that's a bowl of Bibb lettuce and tomatoes.

It's not that all stock photography is terrible and unusable—some of it is technically quite good. And if you know what to look for, and very carefully curate a set of them, you can make them work. But in the end, brands are built on ideas, not pictures.

The real problem with stock photography came with the rise of the Internet and the collapse of print media. Given the sheer volume demanded by online advertising and social media—and the pathetically small size of the ad units themselves—the temptation to eschew original shoots in favor of stock was just too great. So stock photography's use exploded and brands inevitably started using many of the same stock photos—and people began to notice. A 2014 piece in the humor magazine *McSweeney's* titled "This a Generic Brand Video" went viral. It ticked off the cliched imagery that had come to define stock ads—high-speed trains, wind energy farms, time-lapse footage of a busy city at night, people laughing for no apparent reason, and so on.

I had a little fun with this myself in a campaign me and my team at Huge, a Brooklyn-based digital agency, created for TD Ameritrade. The client asked us to promote their retirement services. I'd noticed that retirement ads all seem to use the same stock images—men of a certain age who are just thrilled to be polishing boats, building models, and filling out paperwork. So, under the hashtag #RealRetirement we created meme-like ads to mock how our competitors were talking about retirement and ran them on social channels. They were a hit.

Here's the scary part. This campaign ran back in 2014 but I still occasionally spot some of these photos in the wild. Yikes. The bottom line here is when brands started using the same set of standard typefaces, drawing from the same stock photography libraries, and oversimplified their logos—they all started to look the same. Just like zombies.

3

Zombie Brands all sound the same.

In the previous chapter, I made the argument that too many brands today look too much alike. In this one, I'm going make the case that, as they turned into Zombie Brands, too many also sound too much alike. That matters because how a brand sounds is just as important as how a brand looks. A distinctive brand voice, original piece of music, jingle, celebrity voice, or audio mnemonic all can make a brand more likable and memorable.

I don't know about you, but when I'm driving around and spot a McDonald's, I can't help but hear "ba-da-ba-ba-ba (I'm lovin' it)." Same thing happens whenever I see the Intel logo— it's almost impossible not to hear the famous four-note Intel 'bong' (da-dum-da-DUMMM!). When I think of Arby's, I immediately hear Ving Rames' unmistakable voice and badass delivery in my head. And even if I haven't seen it before, when a GEICO spot comes on, I can tell right off the bat just from the tone of voice of the writing that it's from GEICO.

Zombie Brands have forgotten this. It's not even that they're leaving some or even all of these valuable brand-building tools in the toolbox, untouched. When it comes to tone of voice, it's not that they're not distinct enough—they're literally using the same words as everyone else.

The forgotten art of brand voice.

In 2017, Lucian Trestler, a strategist at BBH Labs, noticed something. There were lots of brands using the phrase "Find your (blank)" in headlines. He did some digging and found that, over the previous five years, this one phrase kept popping up everywhere in advertising.

Find Your Beach	Find Your Strong	Find Your Greatness
Find Your Fit	Find Your Epic	Find Your Forte
Find Your Happy	Find Your Hair Happy	Find Your Edge
Find Your Flow	Find Your Fun	Find Your Volcano
Find Your Force	Find Your More	Find Your Essence
Find Your Unusual	Find Your Flavour	Find Your Fave
Find Your Extraordinary	Find Your Naked	Find Your Grit
Find Your Belfast	Find Your Tribe	Find Your Freedom
Find Your Own Lane	Find Your Dancing Feet	Find Your X

(Via Vikki Ross, a brilliant UK-based copywriting and tone-of-voice consultant.)

It didn't take me long to find more. Like a virus, it's still being passed around.

What's going on here? I don't think it's just laziness. I think a lot of this is the fault of poorly-written style guides. Brand style guides are supposed to sharply define how a brand looks, sounds, and acts. They're a brand's blueprints, it's DNA in written form. But pick up almost any brand style guide created over the past decade, turn to the tone of voice section (if there is one), and you'll find some variation of these basic attributes:

FRIENDLY
OPTIMISTIC
CLEAR
HELPFUL
GENUINE

All that's missing from this insipid list is "useless." Seriously, who would intentionally craft a brand voice that's rude, pessimistic, obtuse, and phony? Another "tone of voice" steer that pops up a lot in brand guidelines is this classic:

"We're like that trusted, smart friend who always gives you great advice."

Sorry, that's not a brand voice–that's a content strategy. After all, your trusted smart friend could sound like a foul-mouthed Jewish grandmother from Crown Heights, or a 20-something fashion designer in New Orleans.

So as a result, when you look around at advertising copy today, what you see are Zombie Brands all speaking in the same CLEAR and OPTIMISTIC tone giving HELPFUL, FRIENDLY ADVICE—making their messages less effective. If you've seen the same phrase from a dozen other brands, it's going to be confusing, or at worst, invisible. Treading water in a mind-numbing sea of sameness is not what strong brands do.

Why did brands forget a distinctive brand voice is one of the most powerful assets a brand can have? I blame the Internet. As a company's website became central to its marketing efforts, the website guidelines essentially subsumed the whole brand. Look, there's actually some logic to this—the same logic that led to the severe narrowing of typefaces to a handful of web-friendly fonts. If you're concerned about brand consistency, and you think most people will experience your brand on your website, it is not totally crazy to think you should adopt the same approach everywhere else. And that's exactly what happened. That's why all brands are using the same FRIENDLY CLEAR OPTIMISTIC tone of voice. Those qualities are basically outlining how to write good *instructional* copy for a website—as opposed to say, a radio spot.

Let's unpack this a little more. In general, a company's website has to do a lot more than just "sell" the way a 30-second spot does. It has to provide a lot of information (offerings, culture, key leaders, address, contact information, news, etc.) and that information has to be conveyed clearly and concisely. Even if the site is little more than "brochureware"—offering high-level information about a firm and little else—it has to be navigable, so it requires basic way-finding language. If the website is an e-commerce site, there's all kinds of copy required that should be written in a way that prioritizes clarity over brand voice—disclaimers, shipping information and so on.

Now it's certainly the case that the strongest brands that have done the hard work of defining their brand voice manage to sprinkle enough of it around their websites so they still "sound" like themselves. But it's just a fact that it's not possible—or even appropriate—to sustain that voice in every paragraph, on every page, on every tab, in every button, on every disclaimer.

Think about it this way. Let's say you walked into a hardware store looking to buy an electric chainsaw, and wanted a clerk to help you weigh the pros and cons and prices of various models. If he answered every one of your questions in a performative voice, or with a joke, a rhyme or alliteration—or he sang the responses—that would be weird and annoying, wouldn't it? Same with websites. You go to them because you want detailed information about something or how to do something specific. So to some degree, the stuff that makes brand voice stand out has to take a step back and not get in the way. But what's happened is that clear, straightforward style has crept into everything else. In the same way Verdana wound up on IKEA's catalog, FRIENDLY and HELPFUL became the default voice of Zombie Brands' advertising.

I've heard that song before.

One of my first jobs in advertising was at The WB Network (now The CW). I was originally hired as the music supervisor for on-air promotions, after serving as the music production librarian at Warner Bros. Television. I'd found my way into those gigs because I was a classically-trained composer, having completed an MA in composition after receiving my bachelor's in composition and theory. But after I'd completed grad school, I realized I didn't want to pursue an academic career. I also had an interest in film composition, but found I just didn't have the ability to write lots of music very quickly, which is what those people have to do.

The two guys that ran marketing for The WB back then were extremely picky about the music used in the network's promos. They really gave the selection and editing of music an outsized amount of attention, partially because back then, The WB was trying to reach teen viewers, and my bosses understood featuring culturally-relevant artists in our spots could help in building affinity with that key demographic. But they also believed music wasn't just a background element to a spot—they viewed it as central to a spot's effectiveness. "Music," one of them explained to me, "is 70% of your spot." At the time, even as a musician, I thought that was crazy.

Over the years, however, I've come to believe he was on to something. I'm still not sure about that percentage, but there's absolutely no question music can make or break a spot. Plenty of academic studies have demonstrated music increases attention, memorability, and emotional impact on broadcast advertising. But just watch a commercial that features little or no dialog without the sound on and see for yourself how strangely ineffective it is. Music isn't just an important element on an individual spot, it's an important *branding* element. The strongest brands operate under this axiom, and curate the music they use in their advertising as carefully as my old bosses at The WB.

A signature piece of music, when used consistently and over time, can become a brand's sonic calling card. For years, British Airways used the angelic duet from the opera *Lakme* by Delibes in all of their commercials. United Airlines' "Friendly Skies" campaign had a lengthy, memorable run with Gershwin's *Rhapsody in Blue*. Since 2019, Home Depot has been using that bouncy bass and guitar riff from "Crampus

& Hellp" by Daveocopia in all their broadcast advertising. It's become synonymous with the Home Depot brand, which undoubtedly aids awareness in their broadcast spots.

The problem is so many brands have forgotten the importance of music in a brand's identity today. At some point, brands seemed to stop caring whether a piece of music was previously used by a rival brand. They got sloppy, and started all using the same songs.

Take one example: the 1968 counterculture classic, "Born to Be Wild" by Steppenwolf. It was not only a hit on the radio, it was featured prominently in the film *Easy Rider,* which premiered 12 years before the oldest millennials were even born. And yet, it has been used by dozens of brands in hundreds of ads since since the '80s, including

WeatherTech	Dodge Ram	Apple Music
Target	Jeep	Pampers
Pampers	Ford	Valvoline
Applebee's	Diet Pepsi	Suzuki
Mercedes	Burger King	Nintendo
Volvo	Taco Bell	Visit California

Sadly, this list is by no means exhaustive. But you get the point. You'll notice there are not only a ridiculous amount of brands that have used "Born to Be Wild" in spots but at least half a dozen automakers have done so. And "Born to Be Wild" is hardly alone in its ubiquity.

"What a Wonderful World" (1969) by Louis Armstrong (Apple, Honda, Toyota, Heinz, Travelers Insurance, Nikon,

IBM, Discovery Channel, McDonald's, etc.), "Here Comes The Sun" (1969) by the Beatles (Phillips 66, Coca-Cola, Target, Hallmark, American Express, Microsoft, Pampers, Oreo, Canon), "Taking Care of Business" (1974) by BTO (Office Depot, FedEx, Dodge, Walmart, KFC, Staples, Applebee's, ADT), "We Will Rock You" (1977) by Queen (Pepsi, Coca-Cola, Gatorade, Ford, Nike, Adidas, MasterCard, Sony, Volkswagen, NHL). And so on. It continues to this day, despite all those songs being over 40 years old. It's like brands are all stuck on the same Spotify playlist.

Why did this happen? It could be brands back in the 1990s were all chasing the upper-end of the coveted 18-49 demographic, and to a Baby Boomer in 1995, a song from the late '60s would be nostalgic. So they all jumped on the same classics, and when that proved successful they just kept doing it. But more likely, classic rock from that time period keeps getting used in commercials today because there is no longer a dominant popular music genre like there was from the 1960s to around the late 1990s.

One day I was driving around with my oldest son Allen, who at the time was a senior in high school, and we were listening to a popular tri-state area music station. "Stayin' Alive" by The Bee Gees came on, and Allen instantly recognized it. In that moment, it suddenly occurred to me just how bizarre that was. The Bee Gees wrote "Stayin' Alive" for *Saturday Night Fever*, which came out in 1977, nearly 50 years ago and nearly 30 years before Allen was born. When I was his age growing up in Miami in the 1980s, there were no popular music stations playing songs from the 1930s. Even if some song from 1935 had come on the radio, I definitely wouldn't have recognized it—and it's very possible my *father* wouldn't have recognized it.

The fact is, a broadly-shared repertoire of popular music—outside of a handful of megastars like Taylor Swift, Lady Gaga, and Kendrick Lamar to name a few—simply no longer exists, or at least, has been greatly diminished. Sure, there are a few brands today that take a lot of care in selecting contemporary music for their broadcast advertising that's both fresh and original. But because popular music has atomized into dozens of genres and sub-genres, brands looking to appeal to a wide swath of people are still mining the same catalogs. And when every other automaker is using the same song, that's a serious brand problem. Swap out another branding element (voiceover talent, font, logo, typeface, colors, tagline) and think about how little sense that makes.

Cheap, fast, and easy wins. Again.

Like stock photography libraries, digital media has been a boon for stock music libraries. It is remarkably easy to locate and download inexpensive stock music today, and with skimpy budgets and compressed timelines, stock music has become the default choice—especially since most filmed advertising isn't backed by a sizable media spend and is only seen as pre-roll or on social channels. Hiring a composer requires planning and oversight. Licensing an original piece of music is costly, can take months to negotiate, and is fraught with uncertainty. So, much like stock photography libraries, stock music libraries have been the beneficiary of these trends—to the detriment of brands.

I'm not saying all royalty-free music is terrible. As is the case with stock photos, some of it is fine. But like stock photography, it's by nature safe, predictable, cookie-cutter. The speed and ease with which one can download royalty-free music for use in advertising has made what used to be a stop-gap measure to cover a tight timeline or barebones budget the default choice. The financial incentives against creating original scores for a pre-roll video—or a single video posted on social media—are simply too great.

What this means in practice is Zombie Brands are all mostly singing the same songs. Music, like tone of voice, is another branding element that's been degraded by the digital media ecosystem.

4

Zombified media.

When thinking about a brand, it's only natural to focus on how it looks, and to a lesser extent, how it sounds. Less examined, but arguably just as important, are the media where the brand appears. Usually media is discussed in the context of budgets and reach—which channels make sense for a brand to reach a certain audience, and how much that will cost. But what's often left unexplored are the inherent advantages or disadvantages of these channels when it comes to delivering compelling creative.

I've thought a lot about media because my father was a media guy. When I was born, he was head of the TV department at N.W. Ayer in New York City, and it was from him that I learned how to look at advertising with a critical eye. Dad had a creative mind—he had been on Broadway as a child and, before he wound up in advertising, wanted to be a television director. So he always approached media with a creative mindset. I grew up listening to him critique spots during commercial breaks while we were watching TV. "That spot should've been a :15, not a :30," he'd say, or "That billboard is facing the wrong way based on the traffic patterns," and, if a commercial was just bad, "I guess they couldn't think of anything else to say." Ouch.

The importance of media—its centrality to the creative product itself—was impressed upon me at an early age. As I progressed in my career, I've come to believe the biggest mistake the advertising industry made was the decision by the holding companies to remove the media function from creative agencies, and spin them off as separate businesses. Today, at most large global agencies, media plans are almost always developed independently from the creative. That's a huge problem, because to quote the great Marshall McLuhan, "the medium is the message."

So when it comes to building brands, media shouldn't be afterthought to creative. Its curation should be considered just as thoughtfully as a brand's typefaces or colors. In addition to the target audience, the reach, and the budget, marketers should ask themselves this question about their media mix: "Are we investing in media channels that are conducive to evoking emotion?" This is critical, because making people *feel* something has greater impact and is more memorable than simply *telling* them something. And some media are better than others when it comes to conveying emotion.

What do Picasso's *Guernica,* Michelangelo's frescoes on the ceiling of the Sistine Chapel, and the film *Oppenheimer* have in common? They are all massive in terms of scale. *Guernica* is 11½ feet tall and over 25 feet wide. The Sistine Chapel covers over 12,000 square feet, and *Oppenheimer* is over three hours long. A big part of their emotional impact is directly related to these mammoth proportions.

Sure, you can pull up a snapshot of those artistic masterpieces on Wikipedia or watch a shorter version of *Oppenheimer* on your smartphone. But the fact is, you don't really experience them viscerally until you see them in their original, outsized dimensions. And when you do, you don't forget it.

Zombie Brands rely too much on media formats that make it difficult, if not impossible, for them to connect emotionally with their audience. It's an unfortunate reality that the core digital ad units—banners, social posts, email, and pre-roll—all fall short here. Because it's really, really hard to provoke a strong emotional response when you're working on a canvas the size of a postage stamp, or if you only have five seconds. I'm not saying it's impossible, or that art always has to be big to have impact. If you've ever seen it in person, you'd know the *Mona Lisa* is almost disappointingly small at 30" x 21". It's certainly true that a single post on X (formerly Twitter, formerly good) can make you laugh. One of the most famous photographs ever taken, Dorothea Lange's "Migrant Mother"—which has come to symbolize the desperation of the Great Depression— is about the size of a standard piece of notebook paper, a mere 11" x 8".

But the exceptions, as they say, prove the rule.

Postcards from strangers are junk mail.

Here's why all that matters: emotion sells. Decades of data and research prove it. According to *Psychology Today,* brain scans show that "when evaluating brands, consumers primarily use emotions (personal feelings and experiences), rather than information (brand attributes, features, and facts)." Another study found the most-shared articles from *The New York Times* are emotional stories. Still another found ads with emotional content are twice as effective as purely rational messages. And so on. I don't think many serious practitioners of advertising or communications, even if they aren't familiar with these studies, would question this.

The fact is, most marketers today are too hyper-focused on media formats designed for scrolling, browsing and swiping. Such formats are perfectly fine for quick reminders, offers, or just for staying top of mind and reminding people you're around. But they're limited when it comes to making an emotional impact—the stuff that builds brands.

A helpful way to think about social ads, banner ads, or emails is that they're akin to branded postcards. From a brand you love, a postcard can be meaningful and spur action. From a brand you've never heard of? Not nearly as much. For example, I'm a big fan of J.Crew. I've been shopping there for over 20 years. I can tell you where every J.Crew is within a 30-mile radius of my house in Westchester County, and I've been to all of the stores in Manhattan, including the Men's Store in Tribeca, where I purchased several suits. Every year J.Crew sends me a postcard on my birthday, which is basically a 20%-off coupon. And every year, I use it to buy something and so they get more of my money. But if I received a postcard from some random men's brand I'd never heard of, even if I needed some new dress shirts or whatever, I'm not going to bother—right in the trash. It's nice to get a birthday card from someone you know. It's meaningless from someone you don't.

Because of their modest scale and disposable nature, social ads, banners and emails, just like a postcards, have far more meaning from a brand you've already formed a connection to than one you've never heard of. It's your previous connection to the brand that gives them salience—not the other way around. So marketers should pay close attention to how much time they're spending on making postcards versus making things that actually make the postcards meaningful.

The goldfish myth.

Does it really make sense to invest in larger and longer formats today? I can't tell you how often I've heard these rationales for micro-sized ads.

"No one reads anymore."

"You've got to capture people's attention in the first three seconds or the ad will fail."

"The audience is only half-paying attention so the logo has to be on screen the whole time."

And my personal favorite, "people have the attention span of a goldfish."

If you work in advertising or follow the media business, you've certainly heard that, because of the widespread use of smartphones, human beings' attention spans have been reduced to that of *Carassius auratus*, a modestly-sized member of the carp family, also known as the common goldfish. In advertising circles, this notion has practically become adland's theory of gravity—a foundational explanation for how the ad universe works today. It's something "everyone knows" and is seldom challenged. Well, let's challenge it.

Let's start with the fact that, if it were literally true people had the attention span of a goldfish, modern human society as we know it would collapse in a few short hours. No activity requiring more than a few seconds of attention would be possible. Planes would be crashing all over the world, highways would be closed by practically non-stop fatal accidents, doctors would be constantly killing patients—oh, and almost no human infants would survive because they require near constant attention.

I can hear the retorts now. "No, no, no—that's not what that means," they would insist. "The goldfish thing isn't referring to attention, generally, it's referring to *media consumption* habits." Leaving that gigantic caveat aside (and an illogical one, since goldfish do not consume media), it still doesn't stand up to even the most basic scrutiny. Think about how many times you've heard something like this on a Monday morning over the past decade: "I watched all five seasons of *Breaking Bad* this weekend!" I mean, really. This is an era when *binging*—a verb previously reserved for excessive alcohol or drug consumption—has been applied to watching television or listening to podcasts.

Can both things be true? Can people really have "the attention span of a golfdish" *and* watch 12 straight hours of "*The Real Housewives of Salt Lake City*?" Could a three-hour movie like *Oppenheimer* gross over $1B? Please.

You won't be shocked to learn the goldfish myth came from people who are in the business of selling digital media. In 2015, Microsoft published a study conducted by their Consumer Insights team in Canada, supposedly showing that human attention span had diminished to a paltry eight seconds. It was based on a survey of 2,000 Canadians, and ostensibly studied the brain activity of over 100 people. The "goldfish" study's findings were so provocative and explosive, it spread like absolute wildfire and was picked up by many mainstream media outlets including *The New York Times, USA Today,* and *The Guardian.* The lede in *Time,* under the headline, "You Now Have a Shorter Attention Span Than a Goldfish" summed it up well:

"The average attention span for the notoriously ill-focused goldfish is nine seconds, but according to a new study from Microsoft Corp., people now generally lose concentration after eight seconds, highlighting the effects of an increasingly digitalized lifestyle on the brain."

This study wasn't only widely covered by the mainstream press and absorbed by popular culture, it seemed to come up in just about every advertising conference (and still does!) and undoubtedly appeared in countless presentation decks. Here is a slide from the original study, courtesy of WARC.

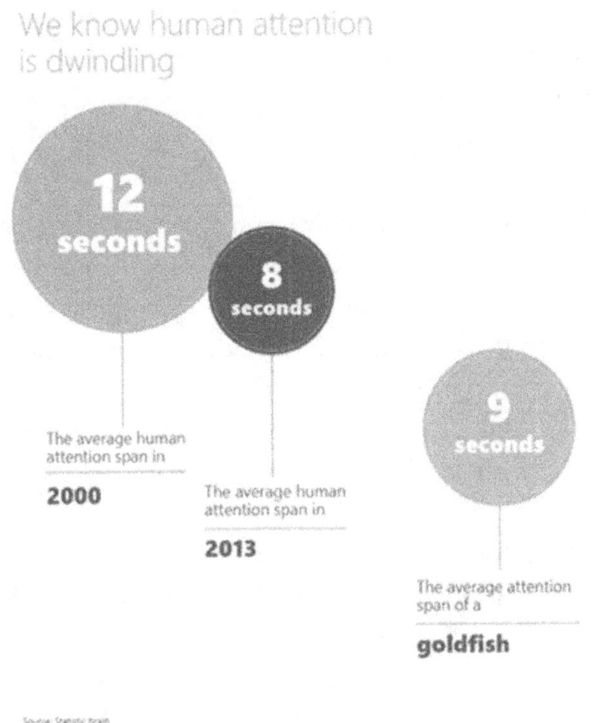

The problem was: it was all bullshit.

In 2017, two years after the "goldfish attention span" myth had already taken hold on the public consciousness, a skeptical reporter at the BBC dug into the original Microsoft study and found that the "eight second attention span" didn't come from the study at all, but was cribbed from a website called Statistic Brain. When Statistic Brain was pressed for where they got that data, they cited another obscure source, which could not be independently verified. Then the dam broke: behavioral scientists and neuroscientists started giddily debunking it. But despite the fact it has been completely discredited, the goldfish myth persists.

There's an additional, delicious irony to this "goldfish attention span" thing: it turns out there are lots of studies that have demonstrated goldfish are actually pretty good at paying attention. To name just one, in 2022, Oxford University researchers proved that goldfish could consistently memorize precise distances. (If only they could change their own water.) It's certainly true that today, most people are more or less addicted to their smartphones. That means smartphones are occupying a large part—I would argue too large—of their attention. And it's true that media formats on smartphones, because of their small screens, are well, small.

Those trends are simply obstacles to gaining attention that marketers have to overcome. And they can be through hard work, the right kinds of investments, planning—and most importantly, irresistible creative. But if smartphone use isn't seen as a specific activity but rather, as part of some innate, irreversible neurological re-wiring of our brains, the argument for spending most of your advertising budget on "snackable" digital media is a great deal stronger, isn't it?

What this means for advertisers.

Hopefully, I've persuaded you that media formats really matter. They're not just vehicles for conveying messages and harvesting eyeballs, they have innate properties which actually shape the messages themselves. Because creating an emotional response is so central to how effective advertising works, media formats which more easily allow for this must be accounted for in media plans. Zombie Brands have bought the "goldfish myth" hook, line, and sinker (pardon the pun), and do nothing but appear in feeds, endlessly hunting swipes, likes, and clicks. That's just not enough to form lasting, meaningful connections with an audience. In the next chapter I'll explain why.

5

Zombies demand you "Buy Now!"

Imagine you're on vacation, in some picturesque medieval town in Tuscany. It's your first time there, and one afternoon, you decide to take a break from all the sightseeing and just stroll around. While you're enjoying an absolutely *perfetto* pistachio gelato, a tiny watercolor painting in old shop window catches your eye. You don't know what the painting's subject was, what kind of store you're standing in front of, or even what the place is called. But it's Tuscany in the summer, it's hot, so you walk in. Even before your eyes can adjust to the indoor light so you can give the painting a closer look, a salesman gets in your face. Without so much as a *buon giorno* he demands, "Do want it or not? 150 Euros, cash only."

I'm willing to bet no matter how much you liked it on second glance, you're not leaving the shop with that painting. Almost no one likes a hard sell right off the bat—especially when you don't even know what exactly you're being offered, and by whom. Yet that's what a huge chunk of digital advertising is today. So many ads we see on websites and social media— from Zombie Brands we've never heard of selling products we don't want or recognize—are constantly demanding we "learn more" or "buy now."

You might be thinking, "Wait a minute. Isn't that the point of *all* advertising? Brands you don't know create demand for products you didn't know you needed with ads." True enough. But this is where my point about media having intrinsic properties comes in. Most digital ads—banners and social posts—are more akin to a postcard or a coupon than a billboard or a thirty-second broadcast spot. They simply aren't great mediums for creating an emotional connection with an audience. They're perfectly fine for reminders and offers, but not for introductions and awareness.

Banners and social posts, like the birthday postcard I get from J.Crew, are designed to spur an action—a click or a swipe, then hopefully (and *extremely* improbably), a sale. In other words, they're a severely truncated form of what used to be called direct response ads. I say 'truncated' because direct response advertising, which when done well can be very effective, was generally long form. Think infomercials and direct response mailers.

This gets to the central contradiction at the heart of digital ads: these units are deployed both for awareness and as direct response, one-to-one ads. But that's just asking too much heavy lifting from that form of media. We've been kidding ourselves they can do both. Here's why.

Trott's Triangle: the fundamentals of effective communication.

It's a question rarely asked: what makes a piece of communication—any communication, from an advertisement for a deodorant to a speech by a politician—compelling?

Dave Trott, a British creative director who had a distinguished career at several New York agencies, had a remarkably simple formula for this I call Trott's Triangle: to be effective, a communication has to have impact, communication, and persuasion.

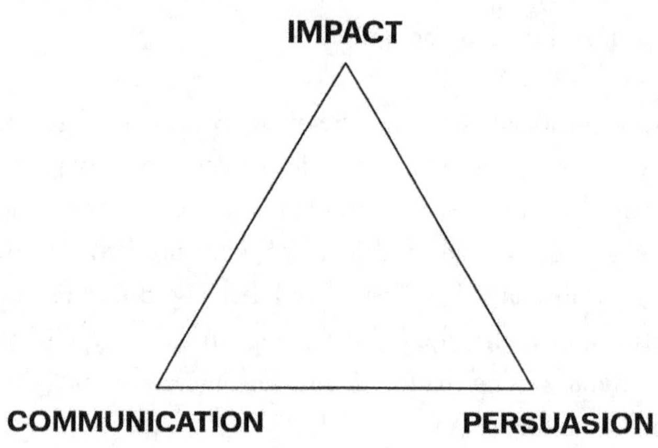

Impact is at the top, as Trott says, because if no one pays attention to it, you've got nothing. It must communicate something tangible, which is fairly obvious, because if the message is not broadly understood, it fails. Finally, to stick the landing, it has to be persuasive—it has to be believable.

Simple, right? Let's put it to the test. Think about some of the most iconic rhetoric over the past century—they all have all three elements in spades.

"We have nothing to fear but fear itself."

"Never was so much owed by so many to so few."

"Ask not what your country can do for you. Ask what you can do for your country."

"I have a dream that my four little children will one day live in a nation where they will not be judged by the color of their skin, but by the content of their character."

"That's one small step for a man. One giant leap for mankind."

I first became aware of Trott's Triangle by watching one of his lectures online and it hit me like a thunderbolt. For weeks, I tried to poke holes in it, but I just couldn't—I found it to be absolutely bulletproof. A few months later, another creative director pointed me to a book written over a century ago in 1915 by S. Roland Hall titled *Writing an Advertisement* which contained a much earlier version of Trott's Triangle. Hall argued "an advertisement has three purposes: to be seen, to be read, to be believed." There it was again.

It seems to me this trio—impact, communication, persuasion, or if you prefer Hall's version, seen, read, believed—is something like the Pythagorean Theorem or Newton's Laws of advertising. It's foundational, immutable, demonstrably true. Yet as far as I can tell, it's not taught in advertising schools or put into practice in any systematic way at most agencies. But when you understand it, it's like a cipher that decodes why certain advertisements are exceptional. All of these ads are just dripping with impact, communication, and persuasion.

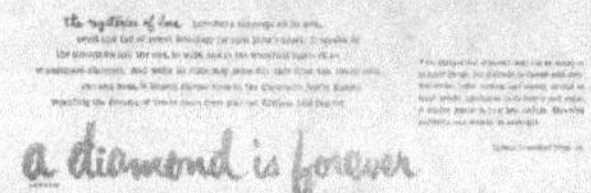
a diamond is forever

Think small.

SOMEWHERE ON AN AIRPLANE A MAN IS TRYING TO RIP OPEN A SMALL BAG OF PEANUTS.

NIKE
AIR
Mothers,
there's a mad man
running in the
streets.
And he's
humming a tune.
And he's
snarling at dogs,
And he still
has
four
more
miles
to go.
Just do it.

This gets to another problem with most online advertising and social media posts. They almost always are lacking one or more of the three sides of Trott's Triangle. Going back to that debacle of an Absolut banner ad from my "How it started/how it's going" series—is there *anything* impactful or persuasive about this?

Or this?

Or this?

Of course there isn't. I'd argue they aren't even trying to be impactful or persuasive. Again, they're simply reminders—postcards. There's nothing wrong with postcards from people you know. But if that's most of what a brand is doing in terms of advertising—if they're reduced to zombies—it becomes a long-term problem. Because they're not getting noticed by or persuading new customers. Not to mention the fact that enough lousy-looking and poorly written postcards, over time, will eventually cheapen the brand.

The folly of chasing clicks.

One of the most absurd aspects of online advertising and social media posts is how brands judge their efficacy: the click. There is a built-in assumption if someone clicks an ad—which is an unbelievably rare occurrence—that it is, by definition, effective. If people don't click, it's not. This basic tenet is rarely challenged. It's taken for granted in our business, and it's a central driver of the entire machine of online advertising. And that's a big problem.

"Well, if people find an ad interesting, they'll click on it," you might argue. My retort to that is almost nothing is clicked—so by that logic, that means no one finds 99.999% of online ads interesting. That's a pretty scathing indictment of digital advertising! But there's a more basic fallacy implicit in that reasoning that, when you actually write out the argument, is exposed fairly easily.

"If this ad doesn't compel people to take action immediately, it is not a good ad."

Imagine if we judged any other form of advertising or communication this way. That would be ridiculous, wouldn't it? I mean, how many pieces of communication actually get you do something right away? There's only a handful and none of them are ads. Your school's nurse calls to say your child is sick. You get a credit card fraud alert. Your bank sends you an overdraft notice. You get an email at work notifying you your password is about to expire. These are all, in some form or another, *emergencies*. People are busy, overwhelmed, and distracted. They don't have time or headspace to LEARN MORE about your organic cotton socks *right now*, even if you spent a great deal of time and effort crafting the perfect Instagram story advertising them. Even immortal ads like the ones above—that have plenty of impact, communication, and persuasion—don't spur immediate action. How many people saw that Harley print ad and immediately went out and bought a Harley? What's more, maybe someone *did* see your organic cotton sock ad, but just didn't click. Does that really mean it failed?

The testing trap.

This binary approach to evaluating ads—if someone clicked it means it's good—can actually be a machine, over the long haul, for producing bad ads. Let me give you an example. When I was global head of creative at *The Economist*, the social commerce team kept running this really ugly, unappealing, social ad. It featured three devices set on a plain white background—a laptop, a tablet, and a smartphone, all displaying the monogram "E"—with some completely straightforward headline—something like "Subscribe to The Economist." Terrible. At the time, I was arguing we should bring back the classic "White Out of Red" campaign that AMV created for the brand back in the 1990s—one of the most celebrated in the history of our business, and one that made *The Economist* famous. Everything I knew about effective communication, craft, and years working in advertising told me this "Subscribe to The Economist" monstrosity was not a good ad. But I was getting a lot of pushback from the social team, who came armed to every meeting with data. The conversations went something like this.

"Why do we keep running this hideous thing?"

"Because it performs the best."

"But why do we need three devices displaying Es?"

"Because three performs better than one."

"OK, but why the boring headline?"

"Direct language like that converts better."

See, over time and through systematic A/B testing, they had constructed all these incredibly prescriptive rules for social ads. Three devices. White background. Straightforward headline. They had all this data to "prove" these ads were effective.

You see the problem. The ad they were calling "the best" was actually only "the best" for a ridiculously tiny subset of the total audience. It was obvious to me all this postcard was good at was generating clicks from people who already knew the brand, knew the newspaper, knew what it covered and stood for, and had finally, at long last, made up their mind to subscribe.

What I understood and the social team didn't was those ads with the three devices displaying the "E" monogram were like my J.Crew postcards. They weren't persuading people who'd never heard of *The Economist*—an excellent product but hampered by a lot of thorny brand challenges to overcome in the United States: its misleading, unhelpful name, the fact it's a British publication covering global affairs, its lack of photography, and its often esoteric coverage. There was no way a postcard was doing all that education and selling the magazine. It was absurd to even think it could. In reality, that social post wasn't an ad at all. It was just a big "subscribe" button for people who already made up their mind to do so.

Two iconic sneaker brands.
One hard lesson.

So maybe you're still not convinced. Maybe you think this is just the way the world works now. Like hamsters on a wheel, people are on their smartphones all the time and brands are doing fine by pushing an endless stream of pellet-sized "content" at them. Besides, you say, it's more efficient to target people who might buy you than fund these expensive campaigns that are hard to measure and don't pay off immediately. Well, that's what two of the biggest athletic brands in the world—Adidas and Nike—thought too. And they found out they were wrong, the hard way.

In October 2019, Simon Peel, Adidas' global media director at the time, did something unusual for the advertising industry. He came right out and said, "we screwed up." In an interview with Marketing Week, Peel admitted that Adidas had over-invested in digital ads, performance marketing, and CRM. He told the magazine:

"We had an understanding that it was digital advertising— desktop and mobile—that was driving those sales and as a consequence we were over-investing in that area."

Did you catch that? Adidas thought it was the digital ads— or the postcards in my parlance—that were doing the selling, when in fact—surprise!—it was people who already knew the brand or wanted to buy the brand. Peel also admitted that Adidas fundamentally misread their sales data, and assumed loyal customers were the engine driving sales when, as *Marketing Week* reported, "60% of revenue came from first time buyers." What's more,

"...while Adidas thought only performance drove commerce sales, it was brand activity driving 65% of sales across wholesale, retail and e-commerce...This was a problem because Adidas' advertising was split 23% into brand and 77% into performance."

Peel conceded the brand had become too focused on short-term sales at the expense of long-term brand building. His *mea culpa* made a huge splash in advertising press—and then everyone promptly forgot about it and went back to business as usual.

Everyone including a brand who should've known better: Nike.

From the 1980s until very recently, Nike and their long-time agency partner, Wieden+Kennedy, have produced some of the most iconic campaigns in advertising history, transforming a sleepy running shoe company in the Pacific Northwest into a global sports colossus. Air Jordan, Mars Blackman, Bo Knows, Find Your Greatness, Dream Crazy. And of course, the deceptively simple three-word idea, executed nearly flawlessly over three decades, which became the company's ethos: "Just do it."

For those of us who work in the advertising industry, Nike is sort of the St. Peter to Apple's St. Paul–the two great evangelists of the religion of brand advertising. That's why Nike's decision in 2020 to turn away from all that and become a direct-to-consumer business was so shocking. The new CEO, John Donahue, would transform the business entirely around a massive DTC ecosystem. No longer would the company produce brand campaigns to drive its wholesale business. They would become a wholly data-driven marketing organization. They would, as I would say it, turn their backs on persuasion and devote themselves entirely to targeting. It's hard to overstate what a radical departure this was. And it was a total flop.

By July 2024, Nike's stock had dropped to its lowest share price since 2018. A former senior brand director at Nike, Massimo Giunco, who had a front-row seat to this debacle, wrote a widely-shared post on LinkedIn, which detailed the shift in marketing. Massimo explained "the brand team shifted from brand marketing to digital marketing and from brand enhancing to sales activation." He added that "most of the (marketing) investment were directed to those who were already Nike consumers," that there was a "massive growth of programmatic adv(ertising) investment," and as a result, "Nike didn't need brand creativity anymore, just a polished and never stopping supply chain of branded stuff." You can see where this is all going.

After taking a wrecking ball to the brand, Donahue abruptly retired in 2024. Elliott Hill, a 32-year Nike veteran who worked in marketing operations, replaced him. An analyst in the *New York Times* succinctly summarized what happened:

Simeon Siegel, a retail analyst at BMO Capital Markets, said Nike's "magic" was that it was the largest player in the sneaker category, with a huge marketing budget.

"Nike is known for its storytelling. When the primary focus becomes on going direct as opposed to telling these stories, some of that magic falls behind," Siegel said.

Nike fell into exactly the same trap as Adidas. They thought they could sustain their global sports empire with postcards addressed to their own fans. They abandoned the hard work of producing messages that have impact, communication and persuasion. They gave up on persuasion and fame. And just like Adidas, they found out that "Buy Now!" isn't enough. In short, they turned into a zombie.

6

The limited influence of influencers.

Long before there was Kylie Jenner there was Lillie Langtry.

Despite what many people seem to believe, influencer marketing didn't start with Instagram. Advertisers have been enlisting popular figures to promote their brands and products for well over a century. In fact, the first influencer campaign dates all the way back to 1882, when an English stage actress named Lillie Langtry endorsed Pears Soap.

Where's the hashtag and CTA?

Of course, before social media, the practice of hiring a popular figure to appear in an ad wasn't called "Influencer Marketing."

As advertisers got in the habit, it became known as "celebrity endorsements." When executed well and over time, the very best celebrity endorsements proved to be not only commercially successful but an effective brand-building tool. Think Karl Malden and American Express, Brooke Shields and Calvin Klein, Michael Jordan and Nike, Oprah Winfrey and Weight Watchers, and a recent personal favorite of mine, Danny DeVito and Jersey Mike's.

You might be thinking something along the lines of, "Celebrity endorsement ads are a totally different thing than influencer marketing because those ads are scripted and staged." True enough. The tone, manner, structure, and media are different. But in the end, they're both operating on the same fundamental principle of leveraging one brand (the celebrity's) in service of another (a product or brand).

Why Jordan worked and Damon didn't.

The most successful celebrity or influencer campaigns begin with a strongly-defined brand. Before partnering with an influencer, brands must first be able to stand on their own. They need to have established their own voice and personality before adding one that's complimentary. Without those elements in place, the brand will inevitably be drowned out by the celebrity. This is really a key point: the celebrity's brand must always play second fiddle to the master brand for the pairing to work to the brand's benefit. The bigger the influencer, the stronger the brand has to be.

Michael Jordan was the most popular athlete in the world, but he didn't launch Nike—and wasn't the only athlete to appear in Nike campaigns. He may have been the biggest star in the Nike universe, but it was still the Nike universe.

When this relationship between the celebrity and brand is out of whack, you get Matt Damon's unbelievably cringe Super Bowl commercial for Crypto.com.

In addition to being a terrible spot for an even worse product, almost no one knew what the hell Crypto.com was—so in the end, the ad became all about Damon. Actually, Matt, fortune favors those who do the hard work of building brands.

When it comes to casting, advertisers have to be choosy about selecting the right influencer who will amplify and strengthen the master brand. There's no magic formula for it, but I think the most successful marriages come down to relevance and personality. Danny DeVito is *relevant* to Jersey Mike's because he's not only Italian American, he grew up on the Jersey shore just twenty minutes north from the original Jersey Mike's— and his playful *personality* matches the brand's. Michael Jordan is *relevant* to Nike, obviously, since he was a basketball player and Nike makes basketball shoes, and his superhuman drive and determination matched Nike's brand *personality*. Oprah was *relevant* to Weight Watchers since she was very public and honest about her struggles with her weight and her empathetic, thoughtful, down-to-Earth *personality* was a perfect pairing with the brand's.

Borrowed interest.

Unfortunately, most brand-celebrity partnerships aren't nearly as effective as the examples above. Far too often, advertisers like Crypto.com don't bother crafting a sharply defined brand over time, then finding just the right blend of relevance and personality to pair with it. Instead, they just grab a popular person—any popular person will do—and slap them on an ad. They "borrow" the public's "interest" in the celebrity to attract eyeballs to their ad. Doing so might result in a brief jolt of attention or even sales, but does nothing to build the brand. Here's a particularly egregious example of borrowed interest from 1927.

What's funny about this is Amelia Earhart wasn't even a smoker. But even if she was, the idea that she was puffing on Lucky's "nonstop from Trespassy to Wales" while attempting to be the second person and first woman to fly solo across the Atlantic is just hilarious. Were people really that gullible in the twenties? Here's another terrible pairing from 1977.

You've probably never heard of Datril, and now you know why. Because when you think of headaches you naturally think of... John Wayne? What? And then there's this really cheesy ad from 1987.

Ah yes, Andy Griffith. When he wasn't winning cases on "Matlock" he was famous for his unbridled passion for... natural dairy products. C'mon Kraft, do better.

You get the point. What these terrible celebrity-influencer campaigns have in common is there's no shared relevance or personality synergies between the brand and the celebrity. They're simply using a famous face for clicks, err, to get attention. What's more, in the case of the John Wayne ad, as one of the most famous actors of the twentieth century, he completely overshadows that obscure, nascent brand. In effect, it's a John Wayne ad and he's selling—oh, I already forgot because I've never heard of Datril.

So the trap of chasing borrowed interest—that the celebrity either completely outshines or is badly misaligned with the brand—is a major concern. One could make the argument using celebrities is best avoided all together. I once worked at a powerhouse independent agency in Austin, Texas called McGarrah Jessee. Back then, McJ as it was known in shorthand, along with GSD&M, dominated the local Addys, and was regarded as one of the best independent agencies in the Southwest. The agency specialized in brands that had a cult-like following such as Whataburger, Costa Sunglasses and Shiner Beers, and consistently made Communication Arts and the One Show. The founders—Mark McGarrah and Bryan Jessee—were so committed to faithfully representing their clients' brands in the agency's work that they had a blanket "no celebrity casting" rule. In their view, relying on a celebrity to gain attention was lazy and by nature, inauthentic. To be sure, that's a purist approach, but the logic is sound.

The nightmare scenario: Hertz, Smithfield Foods, and Adidas.

Aside from the danger of a celebrity drowning out the brand, there's another downside risk to partnering with an influencer: brand safety. Hertz certainly couldn't have predicted their incredibly popular and genial celebrity spokesman would become America's most famous murderer. When Smithfield Foods hired Paula Deen, they thought they'd found the perfect influencer to promote their pork products—until it came out that she was a huge racist. When Adidas inked Kanye West to a partnership deal, they couldn't have imagined he'd later profess to admiring Adolf Hitler. Alas, people are unpredictable.

Even when brands create their own celebrity from scratch, if that person actually becomes indelible with the brand, there's a non-zero chance it could all go horribly wrong. Just ask Subway about Jared.

A delicate balance.

Building brands with celebrity campaigns isn't easy. It requires first and foremost a strong brand foundation and casting based on shared relevance and personality. There's some risk involved. And even if you get those things just right, you have to ensure the celebrity brand remains subservient to the master brand.

That's what's fundamentally different about social media influencers and traditional celebrity campaigns. The hierarchy between the influencer and brand is flipped. The influencer brand is, by definition, dominant and subsumes the brand they're promoting. Whatever it is they're selling, they're mostly doing so in their own voice, in their own environment, filmed in a tone and manner they've established on their own channels. All the elements that make brands distinctive—fonts, colors, voice, photographic style—all of it, are largely absent by design because of the unique way social media works.

Social media influencers' appeal is driven by authenticity, or at least the *illusion* of authenticity. Their followers want to see them behave in a way that's unscripted, honest, off-the-cuff. This creates a feeling of intimacy between the influencers and their followers, and the best ones make you feel as though you're their friends. There's a fly-on-the-wall, spontaneous quality to this medium. As soon as something starts to feel too scripted, too crafted, and too staged, it comes off as fake. The spell is broken.

What's more, too many brands today jump into influencer marketing without having done the due diligence of finding exactly the right combination of shared relevance and personality in a creator, instead prioritizing follower counts. I would argue this not only doesn't build the brand, it actually damages it.

I'm not saying social media influencer campaigns are a waste of time and don't work. That would be crazy. In 2024, they generated over $20B in sales, and the market is growing—though some industry analysts are less bullish and maintain influencer marketing is experiencing a bubble. In any case, what I am arguing is, while influencers might be an effective tool to move product, they're not great at brand building. Of course there are exceptions, especially when the influencer creates the brand, like Kylie Jenner's Kylie Cosmetics. But when brands over-invest in influencer marketing, they run the risk of starving the brand and killing the goose, just as Nike and Adidas did when they over-invested in performance marketing. They run the risk of turning into zombies.

Zombification through stuntvertising.

In April 2006, as the controversial war in Iraq and various scandals engulfed the Bush administration, a grainy handheld, ninety second video of unknown origin seemed to drop out of nowhere and grab the entire country's attention. It appeared to show two hoodie-wearing figures, under the cover of darkness, jumping a security fence, infiltrating an airplane hangar, and spray-painting "STILL FREE" on what appeared to be Air Force One, the president's 747.

"Is this real?" everyone asked.

The video spread like wildfire, in part driven by a new online video platform that launched the year before called YouTube, which allowed it to be shared easily on MySpace, websites and blogs. People, including journalists, thought it was real. The Pentagon launched an investigation. It was quickly picked up by major news outlets all over the world and finally, the whole thing was revealed to be a hoax and a marketing stunt for a fashion designer, the handiwork of a fledgling New York-based advertising agency, Droga5. Thus began the era of the "viral video."

I'm going to pause here for a quick quiz.

If you remember the video or at least are vaguely familiar with it: what fashion designer was "Still Free" promoting? No Googling.

OK, if you knew it was Marc Ecko, congratulations. But since there's intentionally no mention of Marc Ecko in the video (even though he's the one tagging the plane), and since Mark Ecko's connection to graffiti isn't exactly common knowledge either, you'd be forgiven for not knowing that. I would guess only a small fraction of people who saw the video online or heard about it on CNN ever got the whole story. I certainly didn't. Make note of that fact.

Nevertheless, "Still Free" was both audacious and a sensation. It had ingeniously hacked the new media ecosystem of the Internet, generating organic buzz from the bottom up instead of top down. Droga5's case study for "Still Free," which is still online, touts this.

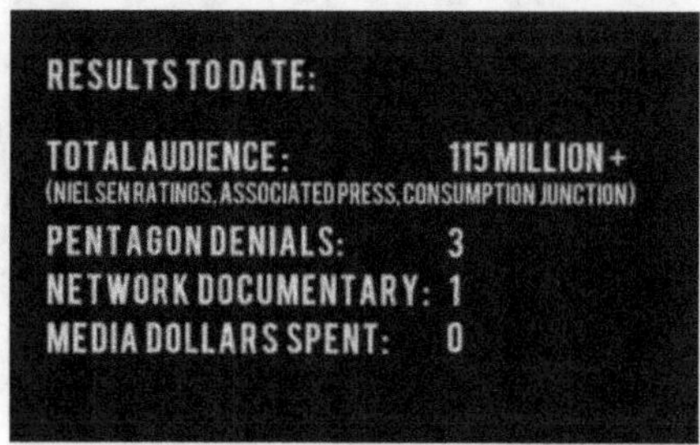

It has been nearly twenty years since the release of "Still Free" and clients are still asking agencies to produce "viral videos"—which is like demanding a "hit song" or a "blockbuster movie" or a "best-selling novel" as though there's a simple, easily-repeatable formula for making such things. The term itself has become somewhat of a punchline across the advertising industry.

ADWEAK @adweak · Aug 19, 2024
BREAKING: Brand's Social Team Celebrates 100th View Of Their **"Viral"** Tik Tok **Video**

⟲ 10   ♡ 28   ⊪ 5K

ADWEAK @adweak · Aug 9, 2018
BREAKING: Client Casually Suggests Agency Should Come Up With Some Sort Of **Viral Video**

⬯ 23   ⟲ 370   ♡ 1.4K   ⊪

ADWEAK @adweak · Jul 12, 2021
BREAKING: Media Director Doesn't Have Heart To Tell Excited Creative Team That Most Of The Views Of Their **"Viral Video"** Are Result Of Media Spend

⬯ 7   ⟲ 126   ♡ 739   ⊪

As successful as "Still Free" was for Droga, in retrospect, I think it was actually bad for the industry, because everyone seems to have learned the wrong lessons from it. The general takeaway by marketers wasn't that Droga caught lightning in a bottle and did something that hit just the right note at exactly the right moment in politics, culture, and the new medium of Internet video, and therefore, the whole thing was probably not replicable. No, the broadly-held view was that Droga had discovered some sort of new formula for how to do advertising in the Internet age: make something cool, post it online, then hope lots of people share it and talk about it—all while spending zero media dollars to support it. I'm oversimplifying that a little, but not by much. It's an attitude that persists in too many marketing departments today.

This "post and pray" approach became even more entrenched in marketers' psyches when brands began to launch their own social media channels. When MySpace gave way to the much more successful Facebook (launched Sept. 2006), Twitter (Mar. 2007), Instagram (Oct. 2010), Snapchat (July 2011), and TikTok (Aug. 2018), brands could suddenly reach a sizable audience instantly. As social media channels and followers grew, the goal to "go viral" did, too.

Another problem with "Still Free," like a lot of "viral videos" that followed is that it was a one-off. Remember, brands are built over time by repetition and consistency. You can't build a brand with stunts alone, because stunts are usually, by definition, *sui generis*. Successful stunts like "Still Free" are quite good at getting everyone's attention, but holding it over time with a consistently-crafted voice, tone, and manner is much harder. Going back to Trott's Triangle, a stunt like "Still Free" might have a ridiculous amount of impact, but arguably very little in the way of communication and persuasion. It's spectacle over substance, by definition. In my view, not only did "Still Free" teach marketers they didn't have to invest in media dollars if the creative was good enough, it also taught them to prioritize stunts over brand building. Social media is wired for stunts.

I saw David Droga speak at the One Club in 2022, shortly after Droga5 was acquired by Accenture. He was very frank in his assessment of the stunts Droga5 had successfully pulled off over the years which built the agency's reputation and he compared them to fireworks. I'm paraphrasing here, but he said something like "The problem with fireworks is that they go off, everyone looks up, and then they're over and everyone goes home." Then he added, "I want to move away from fireworks and get back to lighthouses."

To my ears, this was a pretty big deal. Here was the founder of arguably the hottest agency over the previous decade which built its reputation on splashy activations saying, in so many words, maybe that's run its course. Maybe we should go back to building and maintaining brands as opposed to setting off a bunch of fireworks in the form of stunts. Why? Because without lighthouses, brands become zombies. In the nearly two decades since "Still Free," we've seen an increasing amount of fireworks and fewer and fewer lighthouses. That's partially because of the nature of social media itself.

Social media: wired for stunts and obscure holidays.

Why would a cat food company spell the word "HOPE" on a coral reef? Why would a beer brand install all-white billboards on the roofs of apartments? Why would an investment bank create a bronze statue of a little girl?

The answers: #WorldOceansDay, #EarthDay, and #InternationalWomensDay. Or to put it more succinctly: social media.

Social media is why State Street Global Advisors installed "Fearless Girl" near the iconic *Charging Bull* statue across from the New York Stock Exchange building.

It's why Sheba wrote the word "HOPE" on a coral reef.

And it's why Coors Light got into...the roofing business?

It goes without saying none of these stunts or activations or fireworks would've been produced before social media. State Street, Sheba, and Coors aren't new brands and those "holidays" have been around for decades. International Women's Day dates all the way back to 1909, the first Earth Day was in 1970, and World Oceans Day traces its roots to 1992. So why is this all happening now? Yep, social media.

It's useful to think of social media as a massive river and the organic conversations taking place on it as the direction of the current. If you're an advertiser looking to gain attention, it's much easier to join a conversation and go with the flow than it is to start one by trying to swim upstream. If everyone's talking about #NewYearsEve or #SuperBowlLIX or #RealHouseWivesFinale—if you're prioritizing reach and engagement—it's easier to jump into those conversations and ride the wave of chatter than to start a conversation that's completely off trend. For decades, brands had piggybacked their messages on the backs of holidays, entertainment and sports. But the thing about social media is it became the place where people not only discuss those things but news, politics, and social issues. And social media algorithms elevate conversations that generate conflict.

So brands, eager to set off fireworks like Droga5 did with "Still Free," naturally started looking to activate beyond the same events and holidays they'd invested in for decades. All of a sudden traditional marketing moments in time like Christmas, the Super Bowl, the Grammys, and the Oscars were joined by Earth Day, World Peace Day, World Oceans Day, and International Women's Day. Why? Because there's a lot of organic social conversation around those events, especially by the demographic brands are eager to reach: Millennials and Gen Z.

I'm not arguing brands necessarily shouldn't mark these events (though I do think they need to have earned permission to do so, which most of them haven't). I'm saying this is an entirely new behavior. It's just impossible to imagine a State Street TV spot or print ad in say, 1990, celebrating International

Women's Day or Coors Light making a film about their climate-friendly roofing in 1999. But all three of those campaigns won a boatload of splashy awards and, like "Still Free," a ton of earned media. I'm extremely skeptical, however, that they did much to build their respective brands.

Ask a thousand people to tell you their top associations with Coors Light and I will bet a mortgage payment not a single one will say "fighting climate change." I doubt if five people out of 100 would correctly identify State Street as the brand behind "Fearless Girl"—and even fewer would link the brand with International Women's Day. Ditto Sheba and the health of the planet's oceans. So, in exactly the same way brands can borrow interest from celebrity influencers, they can also borrow interest from events and causes. They can hijack a conversation around a topic—even one that has no relationship at all to their brand—for the purpose of getting attention. If a brand prioritizes spasms of attention over the slow, steady, hard work of tending a lighthouse, they become hollowed out and ultimately, stand for nothing. They become Zombie Brands.

Zombie Brands love shiny objects.

In 2010, when I was at McGarrah Jessee in Austin, a few creatives from our agency were invited by our rival across the street, GSD&M, to listen to a presentation about a new platform that was supposedly going to Change Everything. All our clients, I was assured, would quickly want to exploit this new technology, so we'd better get them in on the ground floor. There was absolutely no doubt about it. This was the next

Twitter. This was the future. I'd attended South-by-Southwest in 2007 when Twitter was unveiled, so I was eager to see what the heck this thing was.

As I listened to their pitch, my curiosity soured to skepticism. What the presenters walked us through was a virtual world, rendered in a clunky 3D, which users could explore with their weird-looking avatars. The thing looked like a fairly low-resolution video game and, as I recall, the "world" you were exploring looked like a nondescript, fairly desolate town, at the center of which was a "shopping mall." The supposed benefit for brands was that they could set up shop in this depressing mall if they bought "real estate" in it, and supposedly, people would want to hang out there and chat with strangers and spend money at all those stores because, well, that was never really made clear. I left the presentation scratching my head. I must have missed something. So back at my laptop, I took the thing for a spin myself. It was boring, clunky, and kind of strange, and I still didn't see the point. That platform was called Second Life. And the industry press had already been downright giddy about it for several years.

"American Apparel opens up shop in Second Life" - *Engadget*, June 2006

"Adidas targets avatars with shop in Second Life" - *Campaign*, 2006.

"A Second Life for MTV" - *Wired*, Feb. 2007

"Coca-Cola to launch on virtual world Second Life" - *Marketing Week*, April 2007

"Omnicom Takes Stake in Second Life Shop" - *Adweek*, Oct. 2007

I don't need to tell you that Second Life turned out to be a gigantic nothingburger. The peak number of concurrent users on the site had peaked in 2009 with a paltry 88,000—less than a single home football game at most SEC schools. Major brands like those above that had made splashy announcements and major investments on the platform gradually and quietly slinked off.

Flash forward over a decade later, to October 2021. Facebook announces it's launching a new, interactive platform which will Change Everything. Just look at the opening of this breathless letter from Facebook founder Mark Zuckerberg:

Meta

Founder's Letter, 2021

October 28, 2021

We are at the beginning of the next chapter for the internet, and it's the next chapter for our company too.

In recent decades, technology has given people the power to connect and express ourselves more naturally. When I started Facebook, we mostly typed text on websites. When we got phones with cameras, the internet became more visual and mobile. As connections got faster, video became a richer way to share experiences. We've gone from desktop to web to mobile; from text to photos to video. But this isn't the end of the line.

The next platform will be even more immersive — an embodied internet where you're in the experience, not just looking at it. We call this the metaverse, and it will touch every product we build.

The defining quality of the metaverse will be a feeling of presence — like you are right there with another person or in another place. Feeling truly present with another person is the ultimate dream of social technology. That is why we are focused on building this.

In the metaverse, you'll be able to do almost anything you can imagine — get together with friends and family, work, learn, play, shop, create — as well as completely new experiences that don't really fit how we think about computers or phones today.

Zuckerberg was so bullish on what the company called the "Metaverse"—which, by the way, looked and sounded exactly like Second Life, he rebranded Facebook as "Meta." Once again, there was a wild stampede of Fortune 500 brands rushing to get in on the ground floor of this new communications platform which Zuckerberg promised would, within the decade, "reach a billion people, host hundreds of billions of dollars of digital commerce, and support jobs for millions of creators and developers." And once again, the advertising industry press showered the Metaverse with investments and attention. Needless to say, none of Zuckerberg's promises came to fruition. The Metaverse, just like Second Life did, fizzled out.

It's not like Second Life and the Metaverse are anomalies. This same pattern—nascent technology or platform announced, brands rush in to exploit it, nascent technology collapses—has repeated itself over and over and over since the first dot com era. There's a ridiculously long list of technologies that were going to Change Everything So Brands Needed To Act Now or they'll be left behind.

If you want to give yourself a chuckle, take a look back on what marketers and the ad industry press were saying about 3D printing, NFC-enabled ads, Google Glass, augmented-reality wearables, 5G, beacons, blockchain, or NFTs. Remember when every brand needed a Smart Speaker strategy because voice assistants would replace keyboards and screens any minute now? Good times.

So what's going on here? Why does this keep happening? Why do marketers keep overestimating the impact of the latest and greatest tech? I think for these four reasons.

First, as broadcast and print media declined over the early 2000s through the 2010s, brands were desperate to reach audiences elsewhere, especially younger ones. So they were all too eager to lap up Silicon Valley hype and jumped headfirst into a lot of platforms and technologies they probably shouldn't have.

Second, because marketers had prioritized generating social media engagement and earned media through flashy stunts, being the first or even one of the first brands to do something "cool" with a nascent platform or technology was a pretty decent bet to deliver both.

Third, in the business world, demonstrating innovation is massively important, perhaps second only to showing growth. In these tech-obsessed times, Wall Street, investors and boards of directors fetishize innovation to the point even fast food brands like Taco Bell and Pizza Hut tout it in their annual reports—as if better pizza is achieved through "innovation." So naturally, CMOs desperately want to be seen as "innovative" by their boards. Think about it from their perspective. If they're being judged by how "innovative" they are, what do you think they'll want to present at the annual shareholders meeting: a beautifully-crafted 30-second spot or say, an NFT-minting kiosk in the Metaverse, staffed by AI chatbots?

And fourth, there's advertising awards. Just as CMOs are required to demonstrate "innovation," CCOs are required to win fancy awards. In fact, many agencies prioritize winning awards over just about everything else. I know firsthand it's all too common for CCOs of large agencies to be evaluated on how many Lions they win at Cannes. Bonuses are tied to it, and jobs are lost for not delivering. And Cannes, just like the rest of the advertising industry, rewards novelty over craft. When it comes to winning Lions, fireworks usually beat lighthouses.

So what's the problem with marketers experimenting with new tech? Well, nothing in the abstract. But there's an opportunity cost to all this activity. Budgets and timelines are finite, and they both seem to shrink every year. If you're constantly running around chasing shiny objects and shooting off a bunch of fireworks because your job depends on it, you're by definition spending less time getting the basics right and tending to your brand's lighthouse. You're less able to focus on a consistent, sharply-defined look and feel, crafting impactful, communicative and persuasive messages in a distinctive brand voice, or connecting emotionally with your audience. What's more, if you're constantly getting attention for things that have little to do with your product or service—as is the case with Mark Ecko and Air Force One, Coors Light and climate change, and State Street and International Women's Day, you're running the risk of diluting your message and therefore hollowing out your brand. You're running the risk of turning your brand into a zombie.

Twilight of the Zombies?

In the first seven chapters, I laid out the case that several overlapping trends have gradually and methodically stripped away a lot of the stuff that makes brands appealing and distinctive and turned them into Zombie Brands. These technological and cultural shifts have robbed them of their voices, dulled their personalities, diminished their looks, and forced their messages into postcard-sized media formats. Driven by the collapse of mass media, and powered by an unprecedented amount of available consumer data, the overall strategic shift from persuasion to targeting has lulled brands into the trap of selling only to their own customers. When they actually do attempt to grab the attention of a wider audience, brands too often rely on stunts and spectacles—"fireworks" in David Droga's parlance—that don't communicate their central promise. Instead they are carefully engineered specifically to light up social media like a Christmas tree and excite both a business community and an advertising press that leaps like rabid ferrets at the first sniff of newish tech.

I know what you're thinking. "Well, it is what it is. You might be right about all this, John, but that's just the way the world works now, and there's no going back."

I've heard many people in the advertising industry say something along those lines. But I think there are plenty of good reasons to be skeptical this current model is sustainable because the scaffolding on which the entire system is constructed—with the smartphone at the center of the ecosystem—is rickety.

Smartphones: the new cigarettes?

Let's start with the hardware, the indispensable centerpiece of the modern digital and social marketing universe: the smartphone. Smartphones are the thing that make the whole shebang work. Advertisers exploit them in a myriad of ways: social media ads, mobile search ads, in-app ads, push notifications and SMS, geo-targeting and location-based ads, video ads, mobile shopping ads, ads in mobile games, and so on. Of course brands can do some of that stuff on laptops and desktops. But as of 2025, people in the US spend twice as much time on smartphones as they do other computers. Think of smartphones as the puzzle piece in the middle of the current media ecosystem Jenga tower. Remove it, and the thing collapses because it's far more central to the current landscape than broadcast television was a generation ago. TV was dominant but there were also robust audiences in print and radio. On smartphones, all three mediums—video, audio, the written word—have collapsed into one small device. That's a whole lot of marketing eggs to put in a single basket. But no worries, smartphones aren't going anywhere, right? I wouldn't bet on it.

Consider this. In 1970, about 60M Americans read daily newspapers—over 30% of the population. In 2010, that number had collapsed to 40M—just over 12%. In 1980, Americans bought over 200M LP records. By 2000, only 1.5M were sold. In 1980, Americans watched an average of seven hours of broadcast television per day. That number had cratered to around two by 2022.

You get the point. I doubt many advertisers in 1990 believed newspaper readership—which had held perfectly steady since Dwight Eisenhower was in the White House—would completely fall off a cliff just a decade later. But that's exactly what happened. The point is, no media is safe from disruption. There's another reason to be bearish about the staying power of smartphones: the increasing sense that they are addictive and causing harm—especially among the generations prized by advertisers, young people.

First, there's smartphones' effect on learning. A 2024 poll by Pew Research found 72% of high school teachers said that smartphone distraction was a "major problem" in the classroom. Many studies have linked smartphone use to decreased test scores. And school districts have begun to respond. According to the Kaiser Family Foundation, as of December 2024, eight states—California, Florida, Indiana, Louisiana, Minnesota, Ohio, South Carolina, and Virginia—had banned or severely restricted smartphone use in schools. Another 15 states have passed regulations curtailing smartphone use in schools. In January 2025, New York's governor, Kathy Hochul, announced a plan to ban smartphones in New York public schools, including in the nation's largest school district, New York City.

Then there's smartphones' effect on teenagers' mental health. According to *The Guardian*, a 2024 study in the United Kingdom found that,

"Teenagers who fall prey to 'problematic smartphone use' are more likely to suffer from insomnia, anxiety and depression, a new study suggests. About one in five teenagers aged 16-18 displayed problematic behavior with their phones, with many saying they wanted help cutting down, experts from King's College London found."

In the hands of the cruel—and teenagers can obviously be quite cruel—smartphones can be weaponized. According to Pew Research, 46% of American teenagers have reported being victimized by cyberbullying. There's also evidence smartphone use has led to social isolation among teens. How else would you explain this (via *The Atlantic*)?

Less-Social Teens

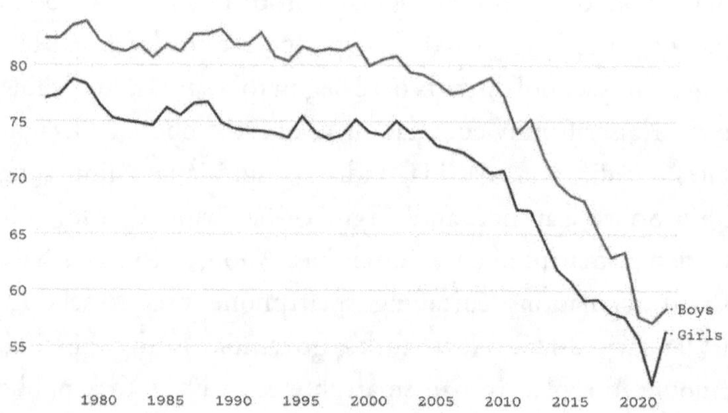

Source: Data from Monitoring the Future, compiled and analyzed by Jean M. Twenge, author of *Generations*

In response, there's a growing movement of Gen-Zers saying "enough is enough" and opting out of smartphones entirely. In December 2022, the *New York Times* ran a feature on The Luddite Club, a group founded by a student at Edward R. Murrow High School in New York City. The idea to ditch smartphones spread to other New York City-area schools and the organization has since become a non-profit with chapters in several states and Brazil with the stated mission of, "Connecting young people to the communities and the knowledge to conquer big tech's addictive agendas themselves." The anti-smartphone backlash can also be seen in the surge of Gen-Z interest in flip-phones. In a November 2023 article titled "Interest in flip phones is exploding among Gen Z and younger Millennials," ZDNET reported that, "new data shows that online searches for flip phones are up 15,369% over the past year among Gen Z and younger Millennials," and added,

"But it's not just flip phones in general that are catching the eyes of the younger generations. Google searches for 'Motorola Razr flip' are up 241% in the last 12 months, primarily because of the company's new version of the flip phone. Searches for 'Oppo flip phone,' another modern mobile phone version, have increased 511% during the same time."

Brands have started to take notice. In 2024, a collaboration between Heineken and streetwear brand Bodega produced The Boring Phone, a vintage-style flip phone with no apps and no Internet connectivity.

It's not just Millennials and Gen-Zers that are beginning to abandon smartphones. Gen-Xers are starting to question them as well. At dumbwireless.com, you can find a wide selection of currently-available flip-phones and plans that support them. New brands like Light Phone, Wisephone, and Sleek Phone have been launched. Just look at some recent headlines, all from 2024 and 2025:

I don't mean to overstate the case. Smartphones are still used by a vast majority of people. They still command a depressing amount of our attention, and likely will for some time. But something's definitely happening, especially with younger generations—the most important to marketers. It's not out of the question to think the smartphone era has already peaked. I also think it's likely, that, in the future, we'll look back on these things the same way we think about cigarettes today. If and when smartphones go the way of the pager—the whole digital marketing ecosystem falls apart. And brands that are prepared for that collapse will reap the benefits.

Anti-social media.

On to social media, those apps that keep people scrolling for hours on end on their smartphones. Social media platforms account for roughly 40% of the average smartphone user's screen time. Yet as I write this in early 2025, every one of the four most popular social media channels—Facebook, X (formerly known as Twitter), Instagram, and TikTok are all undergoing some sort of transition or are in a full-blown crisis. Part of that is due to the fact the thing we call "social media"—a place where you went to connect with friends, family, and the things that interest you—has morphed into something completely different. Even sinister.

Let's start with Facebook, the OG social network. Over the past decade, Facebook has been beset by scandal after scandal. After the 2016 election, I deactivated my Facebook account in disgust. Even though I'd come to cherish what

Facebook originally offered—the chance to keep up with people I knew all over the world, some of whom I hadn't seen since grade school—I'd read far too many articles about how misinformation had spread like a virus on the platform, and how Russia and other nasty political actors had used it to spread said misinformation. I could see firsthand how this propaganda had essentially radicalized people—some of whom were members of my own family.

So I felt vindicated when, in 2018, *The New York Times* reported that Cambridge Analytica, a British political consulting firm, had illegally harvested tens of millions of users' data in the service of Donald Trump's presidential campaign. Although Facebook's android-like founder, Mark Zuckerberg, initially responded by robotically apologizing for the breach, the company's actions belied his simulated crocodile tears.

By 2021, they went so far as to suspend the accounts of a pair of NYU academic researchers who had been studying how misinformation spreads on the platform. Another later study, based at the University of Southern California, concluded that,

"...much like any video game, social media has a rewards system that encourages users to stay on their accounts and keep posting and sharing. Users who post and share frequently, especially sensational, eye-catching information, are likely to attract attention.

Due to the reward-based learning systems on social media, users form habits of sharing information that gets recognition from others. Once habits form, information sharing is automatically

activated by cues on the platform without users considering critical response outcomes, such as spreading misinformation."

In other words, wrote Wendy Wood, emerita Provost Professor of psychology and business at USC, "Misinformation is really a function of the structure of the social media sites themselves." What that means is the spread of misinformation is a feature, not a bug, of Facebook. In the wake of the 2024 election, Zuckerberg went all in on the toxic politics of Trumpism. He not only scrapped fact-checking on the platform, he loosened the site's restrictions on hate speech, specifically citing the election as the reason.

Making bigotry and fake news the twin pillars of your business model isn't exactly the path to attracting a growing audience—especially with Gen-Z and Gen-Alpha. According to Vox, Facebook began losing users in 2022, and the bleeding hasn't stopped. Facebook has basically become a message board for old people. Gen-Z and Gen-Alpha just aren't into it, and I can see why. When I reactivated my account in 2020 for some volunteer work, I was shocked—I hardly recognized my feed. Four years earlier, it had been an endless scroll of people I knew—with the occasional ad or random piece of suggested content thrown in. But now, the experience had been completely turned upside down. All I saw was a bunch of garbage the algorithm thought I would click on, an endless stream of AI-generated slop, with a sporadic post from a friend thrown in, seemingly by accident. It's hard to see why anyone who hadn't joined Facebook years ago would want to spend a lot of time there today.

That brings us to the other major Meta property, Instagram. Facebook acquired Instagram in 2012 for $1B, which turned out to be a very wise investment. Unlike Facebook, Instagram still attracts a younger audience—over 60% of its active users are under the age of 34, and over 85% are younger than 45. But in the subsequent decade, Insta, as the kids call it, has also been rocked by a series of bombshell revelations and scandals. Most alarming, a plethora of studies have shown the platform's use contributes to low self-esteem and mental health challenges, especially among teen girls. The company's own researchers found in 2020 that, "Thirty-two percent of teen girls said that when they felt bad about their bodies, Instagram made them feel worse." The report, obtained by the Wall Street Journal ("Facebook Knows Instagram Is Toxic for Teen Girls, Company Documents Show" - 9/14/21), also found that girls "often feel 'addicted' and know what they're seeing is bad for their mental health but feel unable to stop themselves." In 2023, 33 states sued Meta after an alarming report in the Wall Street Journal revealed Instagram Reels was serving up "sexualized child content." So far Insta, unlike Facebook, has managed to maintain its grip on younger demographics. But for how much longer?

What happened to Twitter after the world's richest man bought the company in 2022 makes the scandals at Facebook and Instagram seem like a few minor glitches by comparison. Under Elon Musk, "X" as he rebranded it, has become a playground for crypto-scam artists, incels and Nazis—a cesspool of misinformation, racism, misogyny, and conspiracy theories, many shared and boosted by Musk himself. Just a sample of the garbage he's shared with his over 200M followers since he took over the platform: Covid-19 and vaccine skepticism, the

"Pizzagate 2.0" conspiracy theory accusing a cabal of global leaders of being involved in a child sex-ring operation, the racist "Great Replacement Theory," climate change denial, the theory the FBI was involved in the January 6 attack on the Capitol, and on and on. As a result, most major brands almost immediately began abandoning the platform due to brand safety concerns, and Musk's telling advertisers to "go fuck yourself" in November 2023—surprisingly!—did not bring them back. This was all before Musk joined the Trump administration and started gutting aid for starving children. Thanks to Musk, X is simply no longer a viable option for major advertisers to reach a wide, mainstream audience.

Finally, there's the cool new kid on social media's block, TikTok. The highly-addictive, algorithm-driven video platform was introduced in the United States in 2018 and subsequently took off like a rocket.

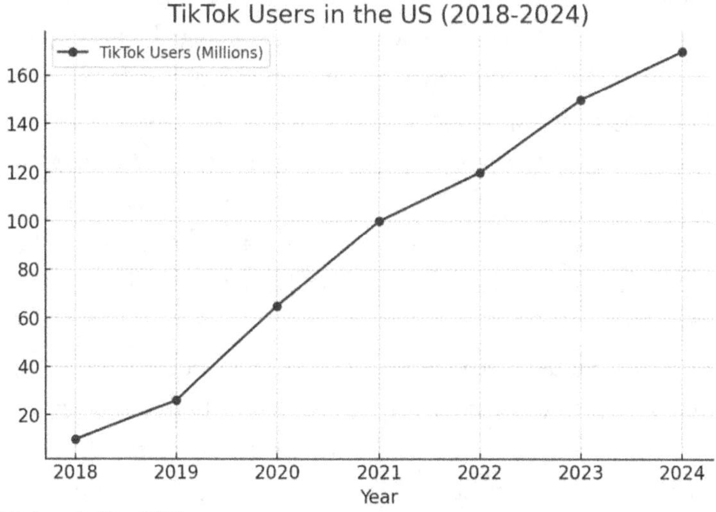

Made with ChatGPT

It's that staggering growth that influenced the other social channels to adopt a more engagement-based, algorithmic experience, in which content a user engages with causes the platform to serve up more of the same type of content. The competing platforms also launched knock-offs: Instagram and Facebook introduced Reels while YouTube created Shorts. What makes TikTok so engaging is that it always seem to know what you want to watch, before you see it. The algorithm is its secret sauce. And that algorithm is owned by the Chinese government.

Which brings us to the big question about TikTok's future. In 2024, ostensibly due to national security concerns, the US Congress passed a bill requiring ByteDance, TikTok's Chinese parent company, to either sell the platform or face a ban. President Biden signed the bill into law, but nevertheless, the Chinese government refused to sell—which seemed on some level to validate the concerns about national security. Technically, the ban should've taken effect in January, 2025 but Donald Trump, through one of many legally-dubious executive orders, put a temporary hold on the ban. In October 2025, it was reported that TikTok would be sold to another Trump-supporting billionaire, Larry Ellison. Who knows what the future holds for the platform, but if it's anything like Elon Musk's takeover of Twitter, it doesn't seem promising.

The cultural and legal threats to the "big four" social media networks have massive implications for brands. Over the course of nearly two decades, social media—initially a place where companies posted press releases and service updates—has become central to marketers' playbooks. It's given brands the ability to instantly reach large audiences without spending a dime on paid media and has fundamentally altered how and when they show up in the marketplace. What would happen to all those playbooks if social media goes the way of magazines?

"Ad-free" streaming services aren't so ad-free anymore.

While the smartphone-social media ecosystem starts to spring leaks all over the place, there's another segment of digital media that's rapidly evolving: "ad-free" streaming services. Just as smartphones and social media began to take off in the early 2010s, channels like Netflix and Amazon Prime seemed to have discovered a completely new business model, providing commercial-free, premium entertainment for a nominal monthly charge. Their meteoric growth was astonishing. From 2015 to 2020, Netflix saw its subscribers grow from 50M to 200M, and Amazon Prime wasn't too far behind.

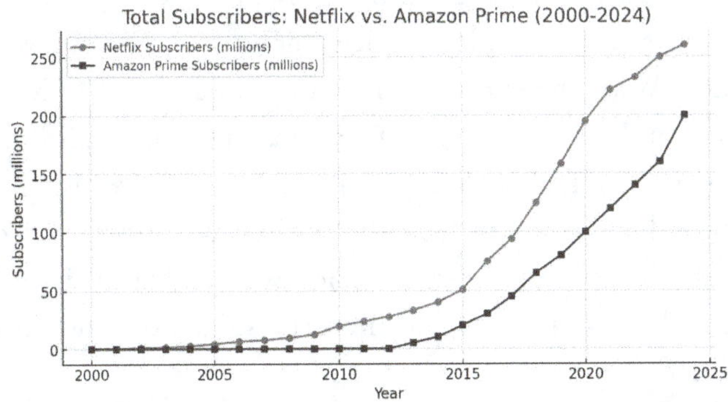

Made with ChatGPT

These services grew—not just because they didn't have ads—but because their programming was better than what traditional broadcast networks were offering. It was better because they were attracting top-tier talent by investing in much larger budgets than broadcast television ever did. In 2020, Netflix was shelling out $13M to produce a single episode of "The Crown" while CBS, NBC, and ABC were spending about $4M per episode on their primetime programming. That's just not a fair fight. Netflix's largesse paid off. By 2021, Netflix dominated the Emmy awards, winning a staggering 44 trophies, a mark matched only by CBS's record-setting 1974 haul.

It was easy to think, back then, that the television commercial—which had been the dominant form of advertising for six decades—might have run its course. It seemed like every other week, some media pundit was declaring it "dead."

But by 2022, Netflix's subscriber growth stalled, at least in part because the streaming service market was suddenly very crowded. With the entrance of Hulu, Disney+, HBO Max, Peacock, and Paramount+, Netflix needed to find additional revenue from somewhere, and so it turned to...advertising. It introduced an ad-supported subscription tier, and the other services, if they hadn't already done so, followed suit. Ad-supported tiers are now the industry standard. And then there's Tubi.

Tubi launched in 2014, but didn't really take off until 2020, when the Fox Corporation acquired it for $440M. Unlike the other streaming services, Tubi doesn't charge a monthly subscription fee—it's 100% ad-supported, just like old fashioned broadcast television. By 2024, it was one the fastest growing streaming services, and the *New York Times* reported that, "(Tubi) now consistently outranks Peacock, Max, Paramount+ and Apple TV+ in total viewing time, according to Nielsen—and is drawing even with Disney+." By 2025, Tubi boasted almost 100M subscribers worldwide. Despite the fact the 30-second spot has been declared dead almost annually for the past twenty years, it is very much alive. What this means is advertisers will have a lot more opportunities to reach audiences with filmed advertising in the coming decade than they did the previous—so they better have something interesting to say. The era of "ad-free" television, which seemed to be the future, isn't. And that could spell trouble for Zombie Brands.

Brands begin to unzombify their appearance.

In Chapter 2, I detailed how in the digital era, Zombie Brands gradually lost their visual distinctiveness, oversimplified their logos to the point of blandness, and started making extensive use of the same pedestrian set of standardized typefaces that display well on computers and smartphones. And because digital media enabled effortless and inexpensive duplication and distribution of photographs—along with the fact the digital media ecosystem requires a high volume of ads in myriad sizes—brands began to rely far too much on stock photography, which by definition lack originality. But there are signs the tide is turning.

Let's take a look at a few brands that decided maybe all of this was a mistake. They unzombified their appearance by tapping into their brand heritage and personalities to refresh their logo and their typefaces. And we'll see how AI visualization tools—even simple, off-the-shelf ones—should be the death-knell of stock photography.

Hopefully, you remember this.

Again, it's just mind-bogglingly self-destructive for brands to intentionally make themselves look like everyone else, especially in a single category. Regardless of what you think of the word marks on the left, they stand out—which is kind of the whole point of brands. In 2023, Burberry finally figured this out.

If you're not familiar with Burberry, it's probably the best-known British luxury fashion brand internationally. Founded in 1856, its iconic tartan has become as synonymous with Britishness as afternoon tea, prestige television and royal weddings. The fashion house's original logo, featuring an equestrian knight on horseback, dated from 1901.

In 2018, they threw all that heritage away in favor of, well, see for yourself.

BURBERRY
LONDON ENGLAND

By 2023, they'd realized their mistake and re-introduced the equestrian knight—as well as a vintage-inspired typeface for their word mark.

BURBERRY

"Burberry flies the flag for Britishness and for the UK and for culture," Burberry's creative director Daniel Lee said at the time. And so it does, once again. The equestrian knight logo is so distinctive, it's just impossible to ignore.

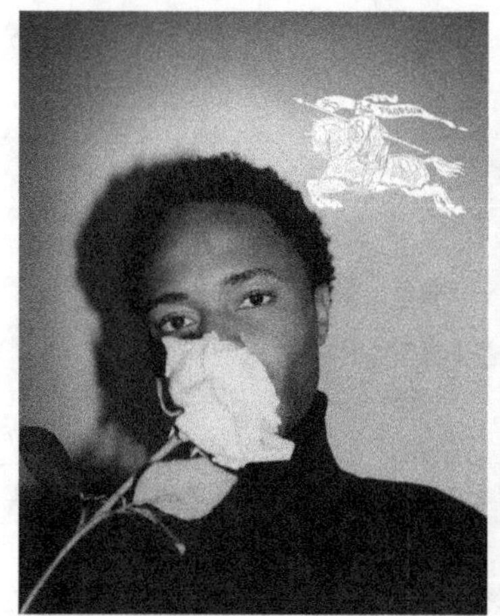

Then there was Yves Saint Laurent. The French fashion designer had been synonymous with an elegant logo and word mark since 1962, which was designed by the great A.M Cassandre. This identity arguably became one of the most recognized in the world.

In 2012, fairly early on in the "blanding" era, the company scrapped all that equity in favor of this dull, Helvetica-based snoozer:

Finally, in 2023, the same year Burberry turned the clock back (coincidence?), the brand reverted back to this:

Tres bien!

Tropicana's $50M mistake.

It's not just fashion labels that have recently rediscovered the importance of maintaining the uniqueness of their brand. One of the most widely-panned and commercially ruinous rebrands in recent memory was Tropicana's 2009 redesign of their packaging. PepsiCo, which had acquired the company in 1998, rolled out this zombified monstrosity with a $35M campaign—and to a howl of critics.

The reaction from consumers was so overwhelmingly negative, *The New York Times* reported on the fiasco. The article began, "It took 24 years, but PepsiCo now has its own version of New Coke." Ouch. It wasn't just that people were complaining about the design on social media—they literally stopped buying the stuff. In the first two months after the launch, sales dropped a whopping twenty percent. It's not just that people were mad about the new packaging. It's that the minimalist design stripped so much of the personality and details out of the original—the striped straw, the various typefaces, the prominent banner "Tropicana" word mark—that it turned Tropicana into a generic, white label brand. The new word mark—yet another lifeless, dull Helvetica knock-off—was hidden off to the side, stacked oddly along the right side of a nondescript glass of orange juice. The whole thing was such a calamity, Tropicana wisely bit the bullet and pulled the new design.

It took 15 years before the company attempted another rebrand, but in 2024, they gave it another go. This time, it successfully gave the legacy brand a modern facelift, while preserving some of its unique attributes.

The "banner" word mark returns, with the accented "i." The striped straw is back. And an orange—rather than a glass of juice--is the photographic hero. All of this feels like a fresh update on the original. New but still unmistakably Tropicana.

Oatly: the most profitable unzombifying ever?

If you haven't noticed by now, I'm a huge fan of the Oatly brand. The brand's visual identity is so fresh and unique and its snarky, self-effacing voice, unmistakable.

What's important to remember, though, is Oatly kind of started out as a Zombie Brand. It's mostly forgotten now, but this is what it looked and sounded like in 2012:

Generic san serif logotype. Flat, corporate blue. Purely rational, straight-forward copy. Stock-ish photography. Pretty much invisible.

John Schoolcraft, Oatly's creative director who oversaw the rebrand, explained the approach, in an interview with The Challenger Project.

"If you look at dairy alternative packaging on shelves; the liquid is always shown, it usually pours from the right hand side, everything is color coded to a pattern that exists in the design world. There are so many conventions. The aim was to get customers to pick it up out of curiosity so we intentionally made these look like we'd just made these in the basement at home. We thought that on every side of the packaging there should be something interesting to read. The legal side on the back we refer to as the boring side. We know that once we're in people's hands, they read the copy, try us, and tend, in great numbers, to like the taste."

A year after the rebrand, Oatly's sales in the US increased 100% to $41M. And it was only getting started, hitting $267M in 2024. The lesson here is that there's a serious ROI on unzombifying your brand.

Custom typefaces make a comeback.

Late into the smartphone era, a few brands seemed to rediscover the fact using a distinct font is a business advantage. Take IBM. Over the past half century, few companies have prioritized design as much as International Business Machines.

IBM's iconic "8-bar" logo was designed by the legendary Paul Rand. The company's mantra, "Good design is good business," was introduced by Thomas J. Watson, Jr. in a company-wide memo back in 1966. That's right around the time IBM started using Helvetica as its primary font. But while that was a bold choice back then (Helvetica was introduced in 1957), by 2017, Helvetica was literally everywhere—and also costing IBM $1M a year in licensing fees. So a year later, they unveiled their own typeface, IBM Plex, inspired by the IBM logo and the Selectric typewriter.

The first time I saw it in the wild, even before I saw the logo beneath it, I thought, "that looks like IBM." That's the branding power of the right typeface.

Then there's Kleenex. When they rolled out a fresh new brand in 2024, they replaced their slightly-modified Gil Sans, a storied font that dates from the 1920s, but which also had grown a bit stale as it had been a system font on Macintosh and Microsoft Office since the early 2000s. So Kleenex opted for a cheerful-looking, custom serif that they could call exclusively theirs.

That same year, Spotify—which had been using a rather restrained, digitally-native serif font for years—ditched it in favor of a dynamic, flexible custom one. You can almost hear the beats.

Brands are wisely moving away from those standard fonts that were rolled out to make the worldwide web more readable and investing in typefaces that reflect who they are.

The death of stock photography and the promise of AI.

Back in Chapter 2, I explained the problem with brands' over-reliance on stock photography. Stock images lack what David Ogilvy called "a story quality"—exactly what his famous ad, "The man in the Hathaway shirt" had.

Stock photographs generally don't have a "story quality" because they aren't produced with an *idea* in mind—such as never giving up even if you're losing, or feeling comfortable in your own skin, or—that if that shirt is good enough for a fellow who looks like he might be a veteran of the Battle of Ardennes, it's good enough for you. And that means they are inherently less useful in building a brand.

Stock images, like stock characters, aren't created to represent unique brand stories. They're mass produced to capture the expected, the commonplace, the quotidian. But here's where AI could make things more interesting. With AI, you can produce images on demand that *do* have an idea. You just need an idea. It took me just a couple of minutes to make this modern facsimile of "The man in the Hathaway shirt" using a free version of ChatGPT with this prompt:

"Create image of a middle-aged man, silver hair and a pencil-thin mustache, wearing an eye patch on his left eye, standing proudly with his left arm on his hip. Wearing a white oxford shirt and brown tie. Standing in a fancy haberdasher. Looking slightly to the right".

I then tried my luck with Adobe Firefly.

These aren't perfect, but with a few additional prompts and variations—or using a fee-based AI—I could've gotten much closer to the original. The power to infuse images with ideas or stories on-demand is exciting, and should put an end to stock photography. Now again, you still need an idea—one that reflects the brand you're trying to build or product story you're trying to tell. But as someone who has spent too many hours of my life over the past two decades poring over crappy stock photo libraries—this is a thrilling development. And it's terrible news for Zombie Brands.

I realize there are serious ethical concerns about the use of AI, and in 2025, polls consistently show people are still queasy about AI imagery showing up in ads. But I think it's inevitable people will gradually get used to the idea that the "mechanic" in the ad for motor oil isn't a real mechanic—or even a real person. I'm not sure they'll be able to tell the difference, in any case.

An interview with P.J. Pereira, AI evangelist.

The advertising industry as a whole is extremely bullish on AI. Large agency CEOs like it because it signals to Wall Street their companies are leaning into innovation. It appeals to the beancounters with its potential for increasing efficiency and reducing production costs. The attraction to client-side marketers can be summed up in two words: cheaper, faster. The advertising press, as I noted previously, seems to greet every emerging tech with an effervescent, almost maniacal giddiness. But there's one segment of the industry that's more skeptical, if not downright hostile to AI: creatives. This is understandable since a lot of the chatter is how it AI will diminish the role of creatives, or make them expendable all together.

P.J. Pereira is one exception. Pereira co-founded one of the most successful independent agencies of the past two decades—Pereira & O'Dell. He's won hundreds of advertising awards, an Emmy, and sits on just about every prestigious advertising board, jury, and committee there is. But one thing about Pereira that sets him apart from other agency founders is he has an atypical background: he's a best-selling novelist and a technophile, having started his career as a programmer. He also founded Silverside.AI, an innovation lab helping shape AI's potential in advertising.

I'd known of Pereira primarily through his agency, but noticed that he started posting regularly and enthusiastically about AI's potential on LinkedIn. I think he's the best person in the industry to discuss the creative potential of AI in advertising, and he generously agreed to an interview.

JL: I think it's fair to say that you are the most prominent traditional advertising agency founder evangelizing the potential of AI. And I'm curious how you got interested in it.

PJP: There are multiple versions of this story. The deepest and longest is actually outside of my career as a programmer. I joined an agency as the "Internet guy" 25 years ago. Founded a digital agency. Then founded an agency that does everything but has a very clear innovation and tech geeky spin on things. When AI showed up, it was a natural fit.

There's also another story. I write novels. And for the last eight years, I've been working on a novel that has AI characters and AI is a big part of the plot. I had to interview scientists, philosophers, programmers and mathematicians because I wanted to make the characters really be a different kind of AI character. Because most AI characters in fiction, they're just humans without emotions. So I spent a lot of time talking about it and trying to understand how an AI being would think. When the book was finally launching, AI suddenly became the talk of the town. I decided to use it to experience it for the book. And then I realized, this is actually going to transform the entire advertising business. So we created a lab inside of Pereira & O'Dell and that lab became a separate agency.

JL: You founded your agency in 2008. That was a year right after the introduction of smartphones and just as social media started taking off. And both of those marked a massive shift, as you know, in the advertising industry. Do you think the introduction of AI is as significant a milestone as those two or greater?

PJP: Way greater. It doesn't even compare. I think that it could compare somehow to what happened when the (worldwide) web was born. But even then it's much greater. I think that comparing AI to social media and the smartphone is making it smaller than it really is. The phone changed our relationship with technology. Broadband changed our relationship with technology. The Internet changed our relationship with technology. All those three things are waves of the same thing. If you think about them, it's like, yeah, there's the internet, then mobile, then broadband, then social. There's this progression of things that are evolution of the same thing. AI is bigger than that.

I remember talking to the scientists and the philosophers doing all the interviews and the research I was doing for the novel. Everyone kind of agrees this is much bigger than the Internet. It's either we just don't know if it's wheel level or fire level or electricity level. The debate between the scientists was that it's comparable to one of those three things, because it is the first technology that actually has a chance to improve itself. We're not there yet, but we're going to get there. We think it's going fast now, wait until the bots start to upgrade themselves. I don't think we as an industry or even as a society have the intellectual ability to understand all the possibilities that will come from these, the compounding effects of this.

JL: When you think about what AI can do for advertising and creativity, what excites you the most about it?

PJP: Right now I would say that the most exciting thing is that this is the first time that technology can help you stay in the flow. Before technology would make things faster and better and help you visualize things, but I had to stop the ideas process and get into execution mode to see it and then come back. And I think that is the revolution from a creative standpoint is the revolution of flow. Being able to stay in the flow and having tools that don't decelerate your flow, because flow takes the flow state of mind. It takes for me about 30 minutes or so to get in the zone, and then 30 more minutes to get out of the zone.

The other thing that excites me in the more philosophical level for the future is what happens when we start to create ideas that have their own ideas, which I'm not totally sure what I'm saying. I'm just saying when you create, if you think of Sam Altman, given a few months ago, saying that he was asked, "So what did you learn from your journey so far?" And he kind of paused for a second, and he said, "I think I always thought of intelligence as something related to humans or living beings or animals. Now I think of intelligence as an attribute of everything," which is a pretty profound thought.

JL: Most of the discussions about AI which haven't been beneficial in my opinion has been about efficiency. About doing things faster and cheaper. I rarely hear or see the creative upside—stuff that actually makes the work better. I'd love to hear how you think AI will help creatives make more impactful work.

PJP: Because of that efficiency, it significantly lowers the risk of trying something strange. If I have an idea that is so strange, but has potential, but it's so strange the likelihood of it working is really small, but if it works, it's going to be great—I can convince a client to do it now in a way that two years ago I couldn't.

Two years ago, I may have needed like a million dollars to produce. Now I'll do it here in my own house, in my backyard, in my phone. I'll do a good enough prototype and try it and then spend a few hundred thousand dollars if they like it and we do it. And if it's not as good, we spent 10% of the budget we would have spent otherwise. That is the creative revolution.

JL: Do you think AI effectively just kills the use of stock photography for good?

PJP: I don't think it kills stock photography. I think it kills lame stock photography. If you just need a person sitting in front of the TV. Okay, I can generate that. It's easier for me to generate than to find it on stock. But there's some great photography in stock. I can still use it. And now I can take that photo and I can make a film out of it. I think what I mean by this is that the photo on stock photography still has soul and is still valuable. But that massive volume of soulless shit that you have there, you can just have an AI generate.

JL: One of the great unfulfilled promises of digital to some degree has been personalization at scale. We have the data, but it doesn't seem like we've been able to exploit it creatively. Is AI the holy grail for that?

PJP: Does AI finally make that happen? I think personalization at scale is an obsolete way of looking at that future. (The promise of AI) is creating an ad that's not only talking to you but actually reacting to what you're saying right now, to what you believe right now, and to what you feel right now, and what you respond is actually way deeper than personalization at scale as we know it.

JL: Is there any part of the creative process you don't think AI has a role to play in?

PJP: Do you know the story about how if you put an infinite number of monkeys with typewriters, one of them is going to write Shakespeare? I think what we're getting to is that it's coming to life. We have a million monkeys with typewriters. One of them is going to write Shakespeare.

The problem is: who is going to find that Shakespeare? I think you can program an AI to go through the infinite number of things and make a shortlist for us. But there's a level of personal intention that still needs to be said, okay, this is great. It's seeing significance. Spotting significance is a human attribute because it has to do with our own personal history. It's like when you walk in a room and it smells like something and it reminds you of something else.

JL: Sir John Hegerty recently posted something on LinkedIn I thought was interesting, especially coming from him because you think of BBH, you think of old DNA, you think of traditional advertising. He said, "stop calling AI a tool. It's more than that. It's a collaborator." Do you agree with that broadly?

PJP: Yeah, one of the worst choices of words that causes a lot of problems that we have to deal with today is the word "prompt"—for two reasons. One, "prompt" implies an immediate response. It's prompt, right? You write a prompt, you have a prompt response. That comes from prompting and writing. But it's hard for our brains not to look at that and see Google. So the combination of two things makes us believe, "Oh, AI is this, I say something and it's going to give me a response immediately."

It's going to give me a result quickly. And that's not what you want from a creator standpoint—that could not be further from the truth. One of the first things I tell my creators when they start to dive into the space is to stop thinking prompting and start thinking directing. Then they get it.

The interaction with an AI is a process of asking for something, seeing something, and then asking for something else, and it just is directing. It's going to allow you to take work you would do in a week to be done in two hours, three hours. But it's still three hours, not a second. You still need to direct that thing. The fact a director directs an actor doesn't mean that director is not an artist, that the only artist is the actor, right? The fact you are directing an AI doesn't mean you're not a creative on a creative task. It doesn't mean you're not a creative, but you have to actually apply your creativity. Just going there, writing a prompt, and post what you have—that's not where it is. There's no intention, there's no belief, there's no connection, no feeling, no soul behind that.

JL: What are you concerned about from an ethical standpoint when it comes to AI as in particular in advertising?

PJP: I think it's a question we're, I'm, not ready to answer yet. I don't think the industry is ready. I don't think the world is ready. Because ethical considerations require understanding of the world that we're living is a social contract. We do not have the consequence of those decisions yet. I can say that, personally, I make a real big effort myself and with my team to avoid prompting things that there goes square into one artist. So okay, if you want to combine multiple things that will definitely generate something that is unique. I'm cool with that. But if you said I want something that looks like

Wes Anderson. But if you find a way to mix Wes Anderson and Salvador Dali with a touch of Nicholas Negroponte, okay, that is weird enough that whatever comes out of it will be unique. Am I taking inspiration in sources or wide enough that you can recognize an ingredient but not the dish. Then, I'm fine. But again, maybe next year, I will have changed my mind.

10

How to unzombify your brand voice.

Back in Chapter 3, I argued that one of the distinguishing features of Zombie Brands is that they all sound the same. Remember this?

```
Find Your Beach            Find Your Strong          Find Your Greatness
Find Your Fit              Find Your Epic            Find Your Forte
Find Your Happy            Find Your Hair Happy      Find Your Edge
Find Your Flow             Find Your Fun             Find Your Volcano
Find Your Force            Find Your More            Find Your Essence
Find Your Unusual          Find Your Flavour         Find Your Fave
Find Your Extraordinary    Find Your Naked           Find Your Grit
Find Your Belfast          Find Your Tribe           Find Your Freedom
Find Your Own Lane         Find Your Dancing Feet    Find Your X
```

It's a shame. Marketers have forgotten a distinctive brand voice can be a powerful tool in building affinity and loyalty, because how a brand sounds is just as important as how a brand looks. The strongest brands usually have equally strong voices that reflect their promise and personality. Here are three of my personal favorites.

Nike's gritty determination.

The Economist's urbane, British wit.

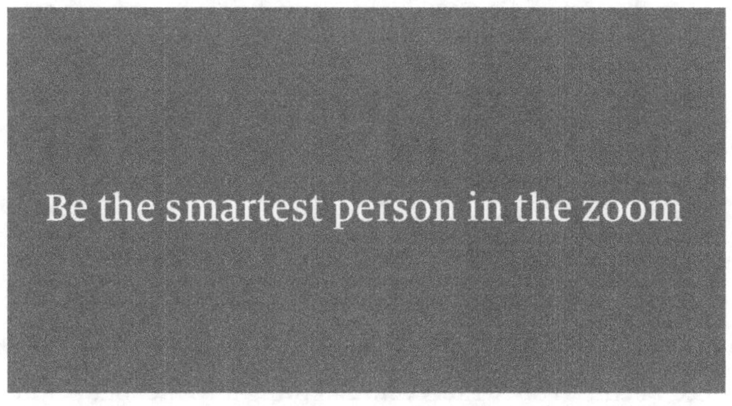

And Oatly's self-deprecating irreverence.

Here's why they're so great. They sound human. They reflect a distinct personality making them very difficult to ignore. They express a point of view. And they're so entertaining they leave you wanting to hear *more* from the brand. When was the last time you thought, "I can't wait to see the next ad from (insert brand)?" That's the magic of brand voice. It builds both affinity and awareness.

So how can brands find their voice again? Well for one, you need talented copywriters who can bring it to life. But before they start scribbling, you have to provide those copywriters with a tangible tone of voice personality they can actually write to. As I pointed out earlier, most tone of voice guidelines are useless.

So here are three different ways to create a sharper, more memorable brand voice.

1. Imagine your brand is a living, breathing human being.

This isn't often done but something as simple as imaging the brands as a real person can do wonders in establishing its voice. Answer these questions:
Is your brand a man or a woman?
Where is your brand from?
How old is she?
Does she have a sense of humor?
If so, is it witty or a bit juvenile?
What is she interested in?
What does she believe?
What does she talk about when she's not talking about herself?

(That last one is a particular favorite of mine, because

it naturally leads to a more interesting content strategy. (Remember Brad from Chapter 1, who only constantly drones on and on about himself? Don't be like Brad.)

Back to imagining your brand as a real person. I think one of the freshest brand voices in the marketplace today is Sam Adams' "Your cousin from Boston" created by Goodby Silverstein. It checks all the boxes. It's distinct and hilarious— and therefore, memorable. Even if you only hear it once, you can easily answer the questions above.

Sam Adams Brand Voice: "Your Cousin from Boston"

Is your brand a man or a woman? Definitely a dude.
Where is he from? Unmistakably from Boston.
How old is he? Late 20s, early 30s, but might as well be 17.
Does he have a sense of humor? Yes, but unintentionally.
If so, is it witty or a a bit juvenile? Totally juvenile.
What is he interested in? Drinking Sam Adams, hanging out with his buds.
What does he believe? He's really not that deep.
What does he talk about when he's not talking about himself? Bro stuff: Pats, Celts, Sawxs, Bruins, beer.

I love that Sam Adams' voice leaned into a Boston accent. In doing so, it celebrates its place of origin, immediately separating itself from, well, just about every beer that isn't from Boston—which is most of them. Sometimes the answer is literally staring you right in the face.

2. Replace generic tone of voice attributes with more colorful and human personality traits.

To refresh your memory, here are some of those boring tone of voice attributes I mentioned in Chapter 3:

FRIENDLY
OPTIMISTIC
GENUINE

These are just too broad, bland, and ordinary to define a brand voice. Why not try qualities like:

IRREVERENT
WITTY
AVUNCULAR

Ask yourself: which brand do you think is more interesting? Wouldn't you want to hear from the latter brand—which sounds like that uncle who always cracked you up with inappropriate jokes, but gave sound life advice? Of course you would.

I realize those particular personality traits wouldn't work for every brand in every category. You might not want to put your life in the hands, say, of a snarky hospital. But take a closer look at how your brand voice is defined, and see if you can credibly swap out at least one of those vanilla traits with a more interesting quality. It's a simple way to take even a modest step away from sounding like a Zombie Brand.

3. Combine two well-known personalities.

A third and final technique for unzombifying your brand voice: take two familiar voices—from celebrities, famous characters, or other well-known public figures, and combine them, forming a completely new voice.

Here's an example. When I was at McGarrah Jessee one of our clients was a high-end, gourmet grocery store chain named Central Market. It's the kind of place that carries half a dozen brands of prosciutto and 47 varieties of cheese. But it's headquartered in Austin, where vintage tees and flip-flops are appropriate dress pretty much everywhere. So sounding too fancy would be off-putting, but you also needed to appeal to the kind of people who like to shop for imported prosciutto and a nutty fontina.

The solution: Dr. Frasier Crane from "Cheers" meets Dr. Seuss. A whimsical epicure, and a delicious brand voice. Here's what it sounded like:

The fellow who came up with this genius technique is Cameron Day. Like me, Cam's a second-generation ad guy. He's the son of Guy Day, the co-founder of Chiat\Day. I learned a great deal from him when we worked together. Cam has written three brilliant books about advertising— *Chew with Your Mind Open*, *Spittin' Chicklets*, and *Stones & Sticks*. He's a student of the game, a real ad gym rat blessed with a restless mind and an uncompromising spirit. I thought his insights about brand voice would make a terrific centerpiece to this chapter. I think you will too.

JL: It's pretty clear brands aren't paying enough attention to their tone of voice these days. Why do you think that's the case?

CD: The dizzying pace of all media. Too many moving parts. The hectic nature of it all.

JL: Why does a distinct brand voice matter at all?

CD: The more media touches your life, the more selective I am about who you let in. I had better want to know you better, if you want a relationship with me. I need to know who you are and what you stand for. Otherwise, you're SPAM.

JL: The counterargument to the idea a distinctive brand voice is important goes something like this: look, advertising is just more transactional today. People have shorter attention spans. They want you to get to the point, so there's less room for personality. What would you say to that?

CD: There's a reason I read the side of the Oatly carton in the stores. I want that voice in my life. What I don't want is more bland bullshit. It's mind-numbing. Entertain me, tell me something I don't know, or get out of my feed. If you're a marketer, you'd better stand for something.

JL: Are there any brands out there today you feel are executing brand voice particularly and consistently well?

CD: Oatly. Apple. Nike. Progressive, with the Dr. Rick campaign, specifically. Mischief and High Dive are two agencies rapidly becoming brands in my book because they generally have interesting things to say on behalf of their clients. Mischief prides itself on calling itself "a safe place for dangerous thinking." If that's not a great brand platform, I don't know what is.

JL: When you began your career as a copywriter, what were you taught about brand voice, and how do you think it's different today?

CD: Brands used to strive to find or want to occupy unique selling propositions. To differentiate. FedEx. When it absolutely, positively, has to be there overnight. Pretty abundantly clear what they stand for. VW. Drivers wanted. (German engineering) Stella Artois. Reassuringly expensive. But more and more, brands seem to want to blend in and follow the same trends. Influencers. Trending memes just a moment too late to actually be relevant. Chasing cool instead of trying to be it for a tangible reason. Parody is the point of difference, I'm afraid. Differences are less obvious. I find it personally disheartening to advertise without having a point of difference. Having a unique selling point is what Apple does so well, IMHO. And when you don't have a unique selling point it's even more important you stand out and be memorable. Progressive and Dr. Rick, being prime examples.

JL: I find most brand voice style guides in today's brand guidelines to be insipid and useless. My theory is that as websites started to become a focus for brands, everything started to sound "friendly and helpful"--because that's what instructional website copy should be. Do you buy that explanation?

CD: I now do work for clients that are trying to bring a unique voice to their brands and their websites tend to be parody drivel. In many cases, it's the first point of contact for someone considering their product. God forbid it sounds like everybody and everything else.

JL: Do you have any favorite examples of a brand voice you had to channel in the work?

CD: I tend to create a persona for a brand and then write to that, or in that persona. It's not my voice, it's their voice, and that voice has to be true to them and their values. There needs to be some kind of truth it grows out of. I cross-pollinate reference points a lot. I look for ways to create a voice that's unique and often that's through a process of experimentation and crisscrossing references and voices.

JL: It's one thing to learn to write in a well-established brand voice. It's another to create one from scratch. Your technique of combining two familiar voices is terrific. Where did that come from?

CD: Years ago, an executive producer gave me a tip I will never forget when talking to music composers. Never give one reference point. Give two and make sure there's a gap in between them, allowing room for experimentation. I do the same thing when writing. For instance, I'll cross an author with a Taylor Sheridan character from Yellowstone, and look for a space in-between so I'm not simply mirroring one of them.

JL: Let's talk about one of my favorite voices you created-- for Central Market. Walk us through the process of arriving at "Dr. Seuss meets Dr. Frasier Crane."

CD: The brand was upscale. But the client was fun. I had the idea of creating a food-obsessed character. Knowing I wanted it to feel upscale yet approachable, I imagined Kelsey Grammar's

Dr. Frasier Crane because he was smart, and well-educated, but still struggled with simple things like relationships. Then I channeled the silliness of Dr. Seuss who talks in rhymes but speaks to kids about loftier things like individuality and self-expression. It was fun to write and it had a bit of a litmus test. If it successfully sounded intelligent but silly, it was inherently right and it's also worth noting that the client genuinely loved the voice, which belonged to me as the writer and Robert Kraft as the voice talent, who was an awesome collaborator. The Central Market voice was written for radio sports and the client never changed a word of what I wrote. The tagline I wrote for them was "Chew With Your Mind Open." They have since changed their tagline so I named my first advertising book in honor of that campaign.

JL: How was this received by clients? Were there any concerns?

CD: They loved it. And I loved them for it.

JL: What makes this technique work so well, to me, is the familiarity of the two voices. If you had just had "Whimsical Epicurean" as the defined voice, for example, I don't think it would be nearly so easy to write to. Is that how you see it?

CD: Absolutely. It's very easy to ask myself two questions: "Would Frasier Crane say this? Would a food-obsessed Dr. Suess character say it?" Two yeses was all it took. Well, that and trying to find something interesting in the in-between.

JL: What are some other successful pairings that you created?

CD: I hate giving actual examples because I actually feel like that's my secret sauce. But this I will tell you. Every writer has favorites and I would encourage people to borrow from their own rosters to create unique voices, so you're mirroring things you have a lot of heart for.

JL: Are there any categories in which a brand voice is necessarily restrained or where it makes sense to dial down the personality?

CD: Absolutely. I think a car account is a perfect place for a restrained voice or a consistent voice. Understated delivery is wildly underrated. I think it would be fun to create a voice that never displays any level of excitement. Sometimes you can create a box and force a restriction. The way out of it can be the trick. I once saw a spot where a golf commentator was whisper-talking everywhere he went because he was so used to doing that on the job. The restriction became central to the idea.

JL: There's a lot of conversation about the use of AI in copywriting. Do you see a role for it in shaping a brand's voice?

CD: Yes, I do see a role for AI. Maybe it's because I have years of practice giving creative direction. Prompting AI is no different from prompting a young, anxious to please team. I know AI can't write it like I can, but it can help. AI helps me rapidly ideate and prove out an idea in minutes instead of hours. As for the ethical implications, I see AI as an ethical threat in the hands of unethical people. And a great tool in the hands of capable creatives. It's just that simple and just that complex.

How AI can help your brand voice sound more human.

I share Cam's enthusiasm for using AI, not as a copywriter, but as a copywriter's assistant. Because let's face it, AI couldn't write this:

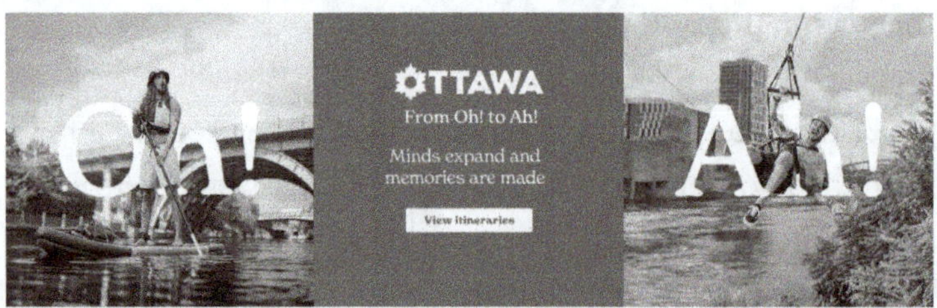

Or these:

(These excellent examples were found in the wild by Vikki Ross.)

But I do think AI is a useful tool for copywriting in these five ways: research, word finding, simulating basic group brainstorms, and inspiration.

AI as your research assistant.

First and foremost, off-the-shelf AI platforms like ChatGPT make terrific research assistants. One of the first things a creative has to do when starting a project is to find out what's been done by other brands, especially in a given category. Although the Internet makes this much easier than it ever was before, the specifics of advertising campaigns—brand taglines, music selection, and larger campaign themes—can be difficult and hugely time consuming to track down. Not anymore.

Let's say you're working on a tagline for a toothpaste brand. You can prompt ChatGPT: "Name 20 advertising taglines that were used by toothpaste brands."

And just like magic, you get this list:

1. Colgate – "Cleans your breath while it cleans your teeth."
2. Sensodyne – "For sensitive teeth."
3. Aquafresh – "Triple protection for your family."
4. Close-Up – "Closer than ever."
5. Crest – "Look, Mom! No cavities!"
6. Arm & Hammer – "Naturally powered by baking soda."
7. Pepsodent – "You'll wonder where the yellow went."
8. Aim – "Take aim against cavities."
9. Ultra Brite – "Put your money where your mouth is."
10. Signal – "The toothpaste with the stripe."
11. Parodontax – "Healthy gums, healthy life."

12. Tom's of Maine – "Clean teeth, naturally."
13. Pearl Drops – "Whiter teeth. Beautiful smile."
14. Zendium – "Gentle on your mouth."
15. Macleans – "Family protection for healthy smiles."
16. Close-Up – "Fresh breath that gets you closer."
17. Crest 3D White – "Whiter teeth in just three days."
18. Colgate Optic White – "Whiter teeth in one week."
19. Signal White Now – "Whitening you can see instantly."
20. Brite Smile – "Confidence starts with a Brite smile."

Now, it's true that you could've assembled this by yourself. But even if you're a super-fast Googler, it probably would've taken you several hours, at least. The above prompt works just as well for sneaker taglines, car taglines, soap taglines—you name it. It also works for music.

Say you've got a great idea for a spot using the song "Bohemian Rhapsody" by Queen. Just ask ChatGPT what other brands have used it, and it will give you this:

1. John Lewis & Partners
2. DIRECTV Cinema
3. IMAX
4. The Cosmopolitan Casino of Las Vegas
5. Pepsi
6. Volkswagen
7. T-Mobile
8. Heinz Ketchup
9. Best Buy
10. Samsung

Is this the real life? Is this just fantasy?

Incidentally, by no means is the above list exhaustive. "Bohemian Rhapsody" has been used in dozens of spots. Just like a hardworking but inexperienced intern, ChatGPT isn't perfect—as it readily admits—and can make mistakes. So you'll want to double-check its work. But for top-line research, it's pretty great.

More than a list maker.

ChatGPT and other large language models (LLMs) can also provide more in-depth information that requires a bit of contextual analysis—for example, campaign themes.

Suppose you were given a brief for a financial services brand— let's call it Freedom Savings & Loan, and the strategy called for a campaign themed around the idea of progress. You could do a lot of desk research, or just prompt ChatGPT with: "List 10 ad campaigns by financial services brands that are themed around the idea of progress."

And you'd get this:

1. Barclays - "We Are All Progress": This campaign celebrated progress in both personal and professional life, focusing on the role of finance in supporting growth.
2. American Express - "Everyday Moments": Highlighting the progress of small businesses, American Express' campaign underscores their role in helping entrepreneurs grow.
3. Visa - "Everywhere You Want to Be": This global campaign emphasizes convenience and progress in payment solutions for consumers worldwide.

4. Chase - "Chase What Matters": Focuses on the progress individuals make in their lives with the support of Chase's financial services.

5. Citi - "Progress Makes a Difference": Citi used this campaign to show their commitment to economic progress and social responsibility.

6. HSBC - "Together We Thrive": A campaign emphasizing global progress, collaboration, and sustainable solutions for the future.

7. Wells Fargo - "Financial Health": Highlighted the brand's mission to promote the financial progress of individuals through savings, loans, and advice.

8. Bank of America - "Better Money Habits": Focused on helping people make progress with their financial goals by providing financial education.

9. Fidelity - "Live the Life You Want": This campaign focuses on financial planning as the means to achieve personal and professional progress.

10. Progressive Insurance - "Progressive Saves": Leveraging the brand name, this campaign underlines how Progressive's insurance solutions contribute to customer progress.

Obviously, this is terrific information to have right out of the gate, since it's clear "progress" is pretty well-trodden theme for financial service brands. You might even decide that you need a new brief.

Supercharged word-finding.

Good writers spend a great deal of time searching for just the right word. This is particularly true when it comes to headlines and taglines, because rhymes and alliteration can make them punchier and more memorable. Since I started using ChatGPT just about every day, it has completely replaced dictionaries, rhyming dictionaries, thesauri, and idiom dictionaries for me. Not only can it find rhymes and synonyms quickly, it can find very specific ones.

Let's say you're writing a headline about a powerful lawnmower and you want a word that rhymes with "grass" that means "win." Just ask ChatGPT, "List 20 words that rhyme with 'grass' that mean 'win.'" And boom:

1. Surpass
2. Outclass
3. Amass (as in amass victories or achievements)
4. Encompass (as in encompass goals or triumphs)
5. Overpass (symbolizing overcoming obstacles)
6. Reass (short for "reassert," indicating reclaiming a win)
7. Class (as in showing class in victory)
8. Bypass (overcoming or sidestepping challenges)
9. Pass (as in passing a challenge or test)
10. Outlast (winning by endurance)
11. Mass (accumulating strength or success)
12. Impress (achieving recognition or success)
13. Harass (figuratively overwhelming opponents to win)
14. Brass (metaphor for boldness leading to a win)
15. Gas (slang for powering through to win)
16. Dash (a sprint to success)
17. Flash (a moment of brilliance leading to a win)
18. Repass (regaining momentum in a challenge)
19. Compass (finding direction to achieve success)
20. Sass (confidence in winning or achieving goals)

"Outclass your grass" isn't a terrible headline for the right brand. Again, a skilled copywriter probably would've gotten to that line eventually, but ChatGPT just gets you there faster.

Now let's say you need a word for a headline that starts with the letter "L" that is related to "connection." Prompt: "List 20 words that are related to 'connection' that start with the letter L."

1. Link
2. Liaison
3. Line
4. Loop
5. Linkage
6. Love
7. Lifeline
8. Logic
9. Leverage
10. Lineage
11. Lock
12. Legality
13. Loyalty
14. Lattice
15. Layer
16. Lamp (metaphorical connection to enlightenment)
17. Latitude (freedom to connect ideas)
18. Language
19. Ladder (connection to progression)
20. Landing (connection point or arrival)

Some are better than others, but you get the point.

Brainstorms on demand.

I have a confession: I've always hated group brainstorms. I find them performative, and at some point in my career, after I'd participated in dozens of them, I became convinced they were terrible at generating good ideas. When I found a bunch of academic studies that confirmed this, I felt vindicated.

What I think group brainstorms are good at is identifying low-hanging fruit—the stuff that's no-duh, obvious, conventional wisdom, just rotting there in a fetid mess on the ground. That's useful information to have, because it tells you what to avoid.

Take a brand naming exercise. Getting a bunch of people in a room and have them free-associate names for thirty minutes is almost certainly not going to produce "the name"— but it will get the obvious stuff on the table, and once you have that, you can write a brief that gets you to more interesting names.

This is a perfect exercise for AI. Because the way LLMs work is they scrape existing sources, known patterns, and conventional wisdom. Basically, they show you what a lot of Zombie Brands are saying. Check out this prompt and result.

Prompt: "List 20 names for a laundry delivery service."
Result:

1. FreshThreads
2. SpinCycle

3. SudsExpress
4. Load & Go
5. Clean Courier
6. WashWise
7. Laundry Loop
8. Pressed & Packed
9. Spotless Delivery
10. FreshFold
11. The Laundry Lane
12. SudsyWay
13. Fluff & Fold Express
14. Crisp Cleaners
15. PurePress
16. WashDrop
17. TideLine Delivery
18. QuickSpin
19. Cleanly Yours
20. BrightThreads

Most of these are obvious (though I admit, if the service was done exclusively on mopeds, "SpinCycle" is pretty good!). But this list took ChatGPT a couple seconds to generate and did it all by itself—as opposed to a dozen people wasting half an hour in a conference room.

Using AI to goof off.

Zombie Brand-speak is flat and lifeless. It has no spark. It's devoid of joy and of humanity. One simple way to avoid sounding like a zombie is to goof off a bit, because Zombie Brands have no sense of humor. LLMs like ChatGPT can help you come up with more human ideas by asking them to do somewhat silly things. For example, I asked ChatGPT to write a jingle about a non-alcoholic IPA, and it gave me this:

(Verse 1)
Feeling thirsty, want a taste,
A brew that's bold, but no need to race,
Hops so fresh, flavor so true,
Non-alcoholic, but the taste comes through!
(Chorus)
Sip it up, feel the vibe,
Non-alcoholic IPA, it's the ride!
Bold and hoppy, crisp and clear,
Enjoy the moment, without the fear!
(Verse 2)
Brewed with passion, brewed with care,
Flavor-packed, without a dare,
Raise your glass, let's make it last,
Non-alcoholic IPA — you've found your class!
(Chorus)
Sip it up, feel the vibe,
Non-alcoholic IPA, it's the ride!
Bold and hoppy, crisp and clear,
Enjoy the moment, without the fear!
(Tagline)
Hop-forward flavor, alcohol-free,
Cheers to clarity — the way it should be!

Then I made it write one in the style of an Irish jig.

(Verse 1)
Oh, I danced through the hills with a pint in me hand,
But me head stayed clear like the cool Irish land!
It's hoppy, it's bold, with a crisp little bite,
But no woozy regrets in the mornin' light!
(Chorus)
Hey! Raise your glass, let's give a cheer,
For the brew with the taste but none o' the beer!
It's a tipple so grand, you can drink all day—
It's a non-alc IPA, hip-hip-hooray!
(Verse 2)
No fog on me brain and no stumble in me shoe,
Just the rich golden glimmer of a fine-brewed brew.
With citrus and pine like a fresh mountain breeze,
It's the drink of the brave, the bold, and the free!
(Chorus - repeat)
Hey! Raise your glass, let's give a cheer,
For the brew with the taste but none o' the beer!
It's a tipple so grand, you can drink all day—
It's a non-alc IPA, hip-hip-hooray!
(Outro - spoken with flair)
So jig 'til the sunrise, sing loud and play—
With a non-alc IPA, we're dancin' all day!

Ridiculous, yes. But maybe there's a fragment of a headline in there. Maybe "Hops without the headspin" leads you somewhere—it's not a terrible line. The point is, you can use AI for more than fact-finding. You can use it creatively as a means to spark more creative ideas. And that becomes another weapon to kill Zombie Brands.

11

Media formats that zombies hate.

Back in Chapter 4, I discussed the importance of an overlooked aspect of advertising, media, and how Zombie Brands thrive in digital formats like social media posts, banner ads, and emails because these formats aren't great at conveying emotion. This matters because evoking an emotional response in an audience is critical to long-term brand building. Study after study has proven that emotion sells. So let's take a look at four types of media that can pack an emotional punch: out of home, longer-form video and film, radio, and podcasts.

You get more "oohs" with OOH.

It turns out, when it comes to advertising, size matters. It isn't too hard to argue a message that spans fifty feet is going have an advantage over one the size of a nutrition label on a pack of chewing gum when it comes to impact. For one thing, the immense scale just makes it harder to ignore. There's also something about the grandeur of larger formats that make the message feel more important.

I mentioned Picasso's *Guernica* back in Chapter 4, and I've had the privilege of seeing it in person, at the Reina Sofia Museum in Madrid. Of course, I'd seen photos of it countless times before. But in person, it's a completely different experience. It's as though you're seeing it for the first time—it's thrilling. If you haven't been lucky enough to experience Picasso's masterpiece in Spain, here's another example that makes the same point. Think of the difference between watching the latest superhero movie in an IMAX theater versus streaming it on your TV. No comparison, right? The fact is, audiences are willing to take the time, money and trouble to buy IMAX tickets for event movies because that format offers a vastly superior experience to any screen they have at home. We know this, intuitively. It's inarguable. But as advertisers, we don't think enough about what that implies when we draw up media plans. Ask yourself: if your brand is never showing up in advertising's equivalent of an IMAX, what are you missing out on?

In addition to the emotional impact out-of-home's majestic size enables, it has a killer feature very few ad formats have today: it's unskippable. There's no fast forward button, no "skip ad" timer, and no payment tier that makes it go away. It's there every time you pass it on your way to work, to the grocery store, your go-to coffee shop, your barber, wherever. It doesn't annoyingly interrupt whatever it is you're doing. It's just there, commanding your attention quietly and persistently.

Does all of that add up to effectiveness? Sure does, according to a 2025 study by Kantar. It turns out, out-of-home outperforms digital channels across the board.

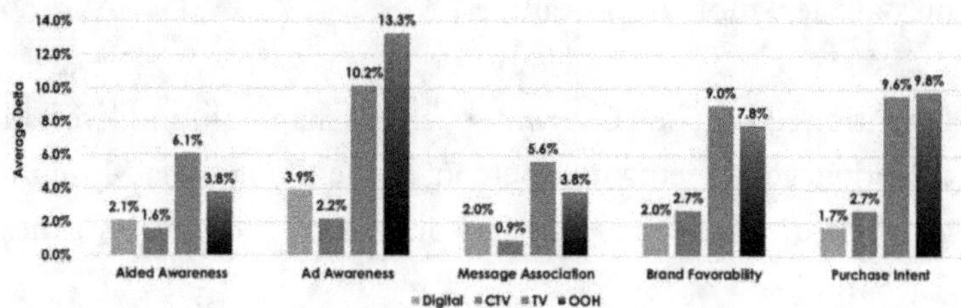

These are eye-popping numbers. It probably doesn't come as a surprise OOH crushes digital on awareness—a product of its built-in size advantage. The larger canvas is better at conveying emotion, and gives the brand a bigger lift in those metrics. It's just more likely people will like a brand that makes them feel something versus a Zombie Brand screaming offers at them.

The other thing that's great about OOH is that, if the creative is good enough, you get more bang for your buck because people will want to take photos of it and share it. The first time I saw this Nike billboard for the "Dream Crazy" campaign featuring Colin Kaepernick, I wasn't walking by the (now closed) Modell's on 34th, I was scrolling through my social feed.

That wasn't a rare occurrence. A 2022 study by the Out of Home Advertising Association of America (OAAA) and Harris found that 67% of Gen-Z and Millennials recalled seeing out-of-home ads in their feeds. The lesson here is that producing social content on the same old zombie media formats isn't the only way to get noticed on social channels. If you make something cool enough in real life—like a killer billboard—it will get passed around on social.

A 30-second spot? How about a three-minutes and 30-second spot?

Throughout *Zombie Brands,* I've detailed a lot of problems digital media has created for brands, but one of the huge advantages it affords is the freedom and flexibility it affords when it comes to film and video formats and distribution. Before high-speed Internet and widely-adapted video players like YouTube, if a brand sought to produce a piece of filmed advertising longer than the standard broadcast media formats of fifteen, thirty and sixty seconds—which were created for the benefit of broadcasters, not advertisers—it wasn't easy to get the thing seen. They could run it in movie theaters (which wasn't as common in the 1980s and 1990s as it is now), produce and distribute it on physical media (DVD), install TVs in retail environments where it could run, or, if they really wanted to break the bank, sponsor an entire broadcast television special. None of those options, though, have the reach and immediacy of the Internet, which is why the juice usually wasn't worth the squeeze. But in the digital age, if a brand has earned a significant following on social media, mass distribution for their film is a simple as uploading it and hitting the "post" button. Even a new brand can strike gold if their film is entertaining enough. Take the 93-second launch video for Dollar Shave Club ("Our Blades Are Fucking Great"). It generated over 12,000 orders in a scant 48 hours.

OK, so the question you're probably asking is: why are longer formats preferred to short ones? The truth is, they're not—necessarily. An excellent :15 is superior to a dull :60. What they are better at, however, is conveying emotion—making people feel something. It's just easier to do when you have more time, and next to impossible if you don't have enough.

Take a recent example. Volvo is a brand that, over the years, has consistently produced terrific long-form films emphasizing their commitment to safety. In September 2024, they released 3-minute and 49-second film for the new EX90 on Instagram—a platform usually reserved for "snackable" videos. (How many times have you heard that "best practices" dictate that social videos be short?) Directed by Hoyte Van Hoytema, the cinematographer who collaborated with Christopher Nolan on *Intersteller* and *Oppenheimer,* it told a "what if" story about a father reflecting on his unborn daughter.

Take a moment and watch it—just Google 'Volvo EX90 For Life film.' Trust me, it's worth it.

The film generated over 121K "likes" on Instagram, and over 1M views on YouTube. There's so much to love about it, and I could spend a chapter explaining why it's so good. But the point I want to make here is simple: can you imagine that film working in 30 seconds? I can't. Even at 60 seconds, it wouldn't nearly have the same impact. And the thought of successfully cramming it into fifteen is absurd.

In the YouTube era, a lot of brands have figured this out and spend a significant chunk of their marketing dollars on what amounts to branded entertainment. Patagonia, to name just one, has produced an entire library of lavishly-produced films about the outdoors and sustainability. The films, over 60 and counting, are in support of their bold mission: "to save our home planet."

Advertising agencies have also realized the brand-building power of long-form video. The agency I work for, Digitas, has stood up an entire division dedicated to producing branded content. Digitas Pictures has produced films for brands like Sephora, KitchenAid and Ragu that have appeared on Max, Hulu, and Peacock and won awards at the Tribeca Film Festival, and it's lead by Mark Book, a film school grad and PhD. I sat down with Mark to get his perspective on this growing part of the industry.

JL: How did Digitas Pictures come about?

MB: Digitas Pictures was born out of a recognition that brands can't just interrupt culture anymore—they have to create it. We'd been helping clients create long form brand content for years, but we wanted to formalize it into a studio model that could develop, finance, and distribute IP with the same rigor as Hollywood. We launched at NewFronts to signal to the market Digitas wasn't just a media or creative partner—we're now a full-fledged entertainment studio, one that marries brand storytelling with premium entertainment. We are acting as a signal to distributors that our content is of the highest quality.

JL: What do you think are the top reasons brands should invest in long-form video?

MB: First, long-form builds emotional equity in ways short-form simply can't. Second, it drives cultural relevance—if you're on Hulu, Netflix, Amazon, or in a festival lineup, you're seen as a culture creator, not just a marketer. These are also spaces you can't buy your way onto, and some of these environments don't have the ability to traditionally advertise. Finally, it's a long-tail asset. A :30 runs for a quarter and disappears; a documentary or series can live for years, reach new audiences (such as multi-platform, airlines, hotels, etc) and keep accruing value.

JL: What can long-form do more traditional forms of advertising—especially the standard 60/30/15-second formats—can't?

MB: Traditional ads are about compression—how do you get one idea across quickly. Long-form is about expansion into brand ethos—it allows you to build narrative depth, explore tension, and actually reward audience attention. It's more important than ever consumers comprehend why our brand exists; you're not just telling someone what your brand stands for—you're showing it in action through story, character, and world-building.

JL: Do you think BMW's "The Hire" marked the start of the wave of branded content in the subsequent decades or was it something more recent?

MB: "The Hire" was absolutely a generational milestone. It proved brands could create entertainment people actively sought out. However, you can look back to other older mediums such as the start of 'SOAP' Operas on radio, or Saturday Morning Cartoons early on in the birth of television. Another major inflection point came with streaming and social democratizing distribution. Suddenly, brands didn't have to buy their way into culture—they could build their own cultural artifacts. "The Hire" set the creative ambition, but technology made it scalable.

JL: Producing successful long-form film starts with a deep understanding of your audience and your business goals. What do you think?

MB: At Digitas Pictures, we don't start with "what's a cool film idea?" We start with: Who are we? What's the business problem? Who's the audience? Where can we earn their attention authentically? From there, the story strategy emerges. When the creative and the commercial are aligned, that's when long-form works. It's why you'll see us partner closely with strategists, media teams, and client CMOs—not just directors and showrunners.

JL: What are some common mistakes brands make with long-form?

MB: The biggest mistake is treating long-form like a long commercial. Audiences won't sit through a 30, 60, or 90 minute ad like they would to get to the content they want to watch with a commercial spot. You have to make something they'd watch, understand and realize value for, even if your logo wasn't on it. Another mistake is not planning distribution from day one—thinking "we'll just put it on YouTube" isn't a strategy and it's actually a detriment. And finally, underestimating the craft. To play in this space, you need cinematic quality, strong storytelling, and partners who can speak both advertising and entertainment.

JL: How do you address distribution when working with channels like HBO Max and Hulu?

MB: We approach it like Hollywood does: through packaging and partnerships. We're not just selling a brand's story—we're delivering premium IP with talent, production, and distribution built in. That's what makes it viable for platforms like Hulu or HBO Max. And from the brand's POV, the ROI isn't just impressions—it's credibility, association, and cultural cachet. That said, we always layer in a paid media strategy to ensure reach—it's not either/or, it's both.

JL: Do you think the model of brands sponsoring entire shows could make a comeback with streaming?

MB: I do—and in many ways, it already has. Look at what we're doing with clients like Hershey's and Sephora. The sponsorship model just looks different now. Instead of a brand plastered across every frame, it's about being a co-creator, co-financier, and/or executive producer. Streaming has opened the door for hybrid models that combine old-school patronage with modern storytelling. I think we'll see more of it, especially as brands seek ownable IP they can activate across channels. Also, the need for gap financing given content consumption has never been more viable.

JL: What's next?

MB: We're just getting started. We're announcing partnerships with other like-minded distributors and production companies, and we're developing IP that will premiere on major platforms in 2025 and beyond. Our focus now is scaling—building a slate of projects across genres, from docuseries to scripted, and co-creating with our clients to breakthrough culture in ways that feel lasting. The next wave for Digitas Pictures is about proving that brands aren't just sponsors of entertainment—they can be true creators of it.

Video never really killed the radio star.

What if I told you one of the most effective media channels for building brands has been around for over 100 years? It's a mystery to me why more brands don't invest in terrestrial radio as part of their media mix, because it's arguably the very last remanent of mass media. According to Edison Research, in 2025, 66% of American adults listen to broadcast or streaming radio every day, and it reaches over 80% of the population. That number dwarfs the percentage of people in the US who use Instagram (47%), TikTok (33%), Pinterest (27-35%), and X (20%).

Let that sink in. Today, the conventional wisdom is that brands absolutely must have a robust presence on social channels.

Period, end of story. The idea of just blowing off social all together is unheard of—downright heretical. Can you imagine a CMO standing up at New York Advertising Week or Cannes and announcing, "We don't invest in social at all because we don't believe it's an effective channel for us"? I can't. So why are so many brands ignoring a media channel that reaches over 80% of Americans? I think what we see here, once again, is the prioritization of "innovation" and the fetishization of tech across the industry. To go back to my hypothetical CMO who has to deliver an annual report to the board of directors, which do you think will give them more kudos: an innovative use of a Snapchat filter for a Halloween promo targeting Gen-Alpha or a new radio campaign? Which do you think will get a mention in *Ad Age*? The answer is obvious.

That's too bad, because not only does radio provide marketers with that rarest of commodities in the smartphone era—a mass audience—another advantage is it's a medium where critical elements that help make brands distinctive and memorable—brand voice, taglines, and music—still work together harmoniously. Here in the New York City area, I regularly hear sharply-produced spots for a handful of big brands. The tristate area's airwaves are constantly buzzing with "Where doers get more done," (Home Depot) "ba-da-ba-ba-ba" (McDonald's), "We have the meats," (Arby's) "Fifteen minutes can save you fifteen percent or more on car insurance" (GEICO). And the thing about these radio spots is they're rarely one-offs. They run again and again and, over time, build lasting associations. The combination of all that is one of the things that keeps brands from turning into zombies.

The other thing about radio is, because it's been around for so long, it's a medium in which best practices have been thoroughly worked out. Unlike the latest and greatest interactive ad format that Google or Meta is pushing out, we know very well what makes an effective radio spot because we've been producing them and analyzing the results since Warren Harding was in the White House. I'm not saying radio makes sense for every brand in every category, but I do think it's seriously overlooked and undervalued, and that more brands should include it in their media plans.

The unusual potency of pods.

The first podcast I listened to was "Serial." The groundbreaking, true-crime series debuted back in 2014, when I was working at Huge's flagship office in Brooklyn, and it seemed like everyone at the agency was into it. Hosted by Sarah Koenig and produced by *This American Life*, it told the story of Adnan Syed, a Baltimore high school student who'd been convicted of murdering his ex-girlfriend, Hae Min Lee, in 2000, and sent to prison for life. The series cast doubt on Syed's guilt and his original trial, and his conviction was eventually overturned in 2022.

I hadn't experienced anything like "Serial"—audio-only storytelling, produced at that level, as a series—in my lifetime. I remember thinking at the time that I finally understood why audiences back in the 1930s and 1940s found radio shows so captivating. The idea that families would gather around the radio to listen to shows played on a monaural speaker seemed completely weird to me, not only because I'd grown up with television, but because I'd never really heard firsthand what the medium is capable of delivering. So in a way, podcasts are nothing new at all. It's just that "Serial" and others that followed dusted off an old format and breathed new life into it.

Although it was by no means the first podcast, "Serial" was the first blockbuster podcast—the *Jaws* of podcasts, if you will. It hit 5M downloads faster than any other previous podcast, and by the end of 2014, had been downloaded almost 70M times. Advertisers took notice. Podcast ad revenue exploded in the series' wake.

Made with ChatGPT

Today, podcasts attract nearly 160 million listeners in the US every month—more than monthly TikTok users, and they've proven to be an unusually effective medium for ads.

- in 2018, Spotify found that 81% of podcast listeners took action as a result of listening to a podcast ad

- a 2023 study in Sweden covering 32 advertisers across six industries delivered nearly 5x long-term ROI
- in 2025, a Cumulus Media/Westwood One study showed that among podcast listeners, 44% made a Prime Day purchase

Those numbers should make a media planner's eyebrow arch. So why are podcast ads so effective? I have a few theories. The first is, if the podcast is highly engaging—like "Serial" was for me—it commands your attention. Second, people listen to a specific podcast because it's covering a subject they're highly interested in, which dials up their attention even more. And third, native podcast ads—those read by the host—lend a great deal of trust to the ad. A Magna Global study in the UK found that 80% of people indicated they trust ads read by hosts of the podcasts they listen to. Finally, there's something intimate and personal about listening to another human's voice—especially one you trust—qualities sorely lacking in Zombie Brand formats.

12

Breaking out of "Buy now!"

Back in Chapter 5, I discussed the limitations of digital display ads and social posts, and how they're akin to branded postcards or coupons. While they might do a perfectly okay job of reminding your current customers why they already patronize you, because of their size, format, and the volume required in a scrolling environment, they usually lack impact and persuasion (two of the three points on Trott's Triangle, and the two that relate most closely to emotional resonance), and therefore, aren't very good at building brands. I also pointed out the content of these postcards are in part shaped by the pursuit of clicks and A/B testing, both of which have their drawbacks. All of these digital postcards are often carefully plotted along a "customer journey" which dictates which channels get which messages, and when. Hopefully, by now, you'll agree with my conclusion that Zombie Brands absolutely thrive in this environment.

The question is, what can be done about all this?

Sure, brands could make better creative—but that will only do so much if everything else is left unchanged. At the end of the day, they're still postcards. So the answer isn't simply "make better postcards." There's a quote from *The Art of War* by Sun Tzu I think is appropriate here: "Every battle is won before it is ever fought." The solution to breaking free of this closed-loop, self-reinforcing ecosystem has to start with strategy. It's in the strategy that clients agree to what they're saying and to a certain extent, where. It all starts with the brief.

Sharper insights, sharper briefs.

A strong piece of advertising starts with a strong brief. And a strong creative brief starts with strong insights. That's why strategists are constantly digging around for insights and trends that can inform a cultural tension in a brief. OK, I know that sounds like a lot of buzzwords and marketingspeak, so let me explain what I mean in more detail.

The reason a cultural tension is important in a creative brief is because it gives the creative something to push up against and, ultimately resolve, making the work more resonant to an audience. By grounding the creative in a cultural tension, you're tapping into a human truth—something people feel, deep down, but don't necessarily articulate regularly or are even consciously aware of. If you do that successfully, the product or service you're advertising seems to address this unspoken but very real need, almost like magic. That's where the gold is.

Here's an example. Take the Progressive Insurance campaign featuring "Dr. Rick" who helps keep young homeowners from turning into their parents. It's the brainchild of Arnold Worldwide in Boston, and one of my favorite campaigns over the past decade—the writing and performances and accompanying saccharine piano track—are all hilarious. But what makes the work so devilishly effective is what's lurking hidden, underneath—the cultural tension it's resolving. That is, as people settle into adulthood—taking on all the responsibilities that come with homeownership—they feel pressure to assume "grown up" behaviors, while at the same time, they have a creeping sense that they're losing their carefree, youthful 20-something selves. It's a jarring experience for anyone who has gone through it—and a juicy cultural tension—and the results speak for themselves. But mining that particular nugget takes a lot of digging.

The big problem I've seen over the years in creative briefs is the insights that lead up to the cultural tension are often quite shallow, and in my view, not really "insights" at all, but rather banal observations. I don't blame strategists for this, I blame the unreasonably compressed timelines agencies came to be expected to produce work in the scrolling, always-on, smartphone, Zombie Brand era. If you have to squeeze a month of market and audience research into a couple of days, you're kidding yourself if you don't think you're sacrificing something. So shallower insights lead to shallower briefs—which lead to, yep, zombie creative.

This is where AI can do a lot of good. For one thing, strategists can use AI to perform social listening, poring over and analyzing millions of social posts, reviews, and comments at a scale that was previously extremely time-consuming, if not impossible. That can help a strategist identify hard-to-spot sentiments and hidden trends, and mine them for interesting insights.

Another way AI can help sharpen insights is by identifying niche segments and micro-communities to target with creative. That's important, because as I've pointed out, there is almost no mass media left, and I've long been skeptical of demographic-based insights. Sigh, this is getting really jargony again, so I'll pause to explain.

What is a "demographic-based insight"? It's a characteristic or tendency that's *supposedly* unique to a particular demographic—usually an age group. My favorite example from the 2010s was this gem: "Millennials aren't really into buying things, they crave experiences." It became kind of a running joke in advertising circles because it wasn't insightful at all, just a fancy way of restating the mind-numbingly obvious observation that teenagers and college students don't have a lot money. (It's also self-defeating. If Millennials don't actually buy stuff, what are we even doing here?) But you would be surprised how many senior executives and CMO-types nodded approvingly when they heard it, repeated it as gospel, and believed it in their bones. It was right up there with the "attention span of a goldfish" as another one of those Things Everyone in Advertising Knows Is True.

The reason I'm not a big believer in demographic-based insights is because I just haven't seen too much evidence of them in the people I've actually known over the course of my life. Sure, I've observed a few notable differences across generations. Take one example, my grandmother always kept wads of cash hidden around her house because she'd lived through the Great Depression and mass bank failures. But my Mom and Dad, members of the Silent and Greatest generations, didn't inherit this habit. I could name a couple more, but these are few and far between, and they tend to be trivial. I've known elderly people who have the temperament of college students, and I've known 20-somethings who were grumpy curmudgeons. I just basically believe human nature hasn't changed much over the past 10,000 years, let alone a paltry 25. As evidence, I'd point to any epic poem by Homer or Marcus Aurelius's *Meditations* or any one of the 38 Shakespeare plays. People just haven't changed that much.

OK, back to AI helping strategists identifying niche, micro-community segments. Lydia Cox, who leads the social media strategy practice at Digitas (and who you will hear more from in the next chapter), believes we're in a "niche era." In her view, the Internet self-organizes around interests. "We don't organize as 18-24," Cox points out.

"The internet is organized around passions, essentially killing demo-based marketing," Cox told me. She saw the potential for AI to help strategists isolate micro-communities to make creative and media work harder, and was behind the agency's new AI Community Agent project, which does just that.

"Our agent helps teams step outside their own 'for you page' and algorithm bubbles to identify the communities they want to reach: who's in them, what they believe, the unspoken rules, where influence happens," she added.

The G-Class Mercedes crashes into the customer journey.

I thought a good person to talk to about how we un-zombify creative briefs is Ali Amarsy, Chief Strategy Officer at

Digitas. Previously, Ali was the global strategy lead at Publicis Commerce, and also headed up Leo Burnett's strategy and effectiveness disciplines in the UAE. We talked about the complexity of digital media, whether brand houses and customer journeys still mattered, and how strategy can use AI to inform more interesting creative.

JL: You've been at this strategy thing for a while now. From your vantage point, what's the biggest thing that's changed about the business since the introduction of smartphones and social media?

AA: It may sound cliché, but the speed and the time spent with communication, and therefore, the demand on content. We're consuming stuff concurrently. Just the sheer volume of channels.

JL: One thing that's certainly changed, obviously, is the level of complexity. There are so many media formats and channels that have their own idiosyncratic rules and that makes it harder to maintain a consistent voice and look. How has media fragmentation impacted strategy?

AA: I don't know that we've consciously graduated, but I think the brand house is a thing of the past. We used to sit for days, and hammer out a brand house and it was at the top of every brief. The fact that it's so rigid doesn't work anymore. I think now that a brand should be like a framework–like a soccer field. I will tell you exactly what is out of bounds is–do not do these things. Don't poke fun at this crowd, you know? Don't touch this topic. So you understand your playing field – the playing field is what the brand offers paid, owned and earned to play within.

JL: We've come up with various ways of managing this complexity such as customer journeys. Given the proliferation of channels and formats, I understand the need for customer journeys and find them useful in building out a campaign. But they have a couple of big flaws. For one thing, they limit the creative output to the same laundry list of deliverables and that can stifle creative thinking and innovation. How do you make the space for more left field ideas in a journey?

AA: I look at the world as a fluid funnel. Living, liking, loving, and loyal, are the four steps of that funnel and academically, we still have to make sure that we are checking all the boxes, right? But the academic and the theoretical is certainly not how people live. There are four phases to this journey, and you may come in and out from different doors, and you may go back and forth. I'm currently in sixteen different relationships with sixteen different products and brands at different levels and of maturity or advancement. And that's how that works. The funnel is fluid, and it leaves you with jobs to be done, rooted in a barrier.

JL: The other thing that bugs me about journeys is they don't reflect how the mind works and how people make purchase decisions. For example, a car brand's customer journey probably starts with "Joe decides he needs a new car so he starts researching cars." But that's not really how that works. Joe already has a ton of assumptions about car brands he's interested in before he starts looking around. Also, he might be browsing, not because he's buying a car _right now_ but he's just bored and likes cars. Are we thinking too linearly with these things?

AA: Here's a real-life example of that. So the Mercedes G-Class–I lust over this car. And my relationship with the G-class is, if you were to think about the funnel, I'm already in the "advocacy" loop. I'm already in the family, even though I don't own it. And one day, they're going to hit me with the right middle of the funnel offer or the right ad, and I'm just like 'fuck it, I'm buying it', and I'm going to have done top-middle-bottom funnel **after** having done loyalty because I'm in the Loyalty Loop already.

JL: So I guess the tension I'm trying to resolve is, in a fragmented, multi-channel media environment, how do we break out of cookie-cutter deliverables and find room for breakthrough ideas that build brands?

AA: Audience-based creativity and data. We have, at our disposal, 255 million people tracked across 7,000 criteria, updated three times a day, and the confirmation of their behavior is credit card swipes. So it's fact. Add on to that intuition—something we're observing in the world. Then we can make a compelling argument, rooted in the audience, which is basically—look at these people look at their habits— for something unexpected. Something clients might not have known when they made their initial investment.

JL: Another challenge I see with the digital media ecosystem are the self-reinforcing aspects of it, such as testing. I've seen a lot of misuse of testing over the years, propping up ads I know can't possibly be effective. But if you test two really crappy ads, one is going to win—and that doesn't make it "good." How can we approach testing more in a way that doesn't elevate bad work?

AA: I love that. Two shitty ads, at least one of them's going to win, which doesn't mean it's good! It just means it's less shit.

Look, everyone will share the stats on how CMO tenure is the lowest ever, like 18 months. And therefore, you know, they're not looking to make big plays. They're trying to just last to the nineteenth month. So they hide behind data. So I understand why people do that, but as that's happening, there's also like this irreverence for the voice of truth. But what about testing with influencers? Or with your sub-community? What does this group of twenty people feel about it, knowing that if it hits with them, it'll have a ripple effect on others?

JL: When it comes to new technologies such as AI, you've written about how we need to put "magic" in the machines— ensuring there's still humanity that's coming through in the work so that it connects emotionally with an audience. That's music to my ears. How are you and your team infusing that ethos into practice?

AA: I want to leave linear to the machines. Because what AI is going to do is take all of the past informed decisions on what would be the best solution. It's like auto complete—intelligent autocomplete. So let it think linearly and make that a really strong plan B. That's what our agents are able to do today. Seven out of 10 quality—and that frees you up. If you give the linear to the machine, it's your job to do lateral. Get weird. Think about it. Think about a collaboration between Tyson's frozen chicken and Victoria's Secret. I guarantee you it will never happen, but if you take the time to think about that, you will think about new gender roles, about shock value about new distribution channels. You will think about it who's tasked with making dinner. What does that person want? And again, you now have those twenty minutes because you're getting a really strong plan B from your agentic partner, so either you can up-level that or beat it, because ultimately it's going to finding a brilliant strategy by any means necessary. Either use AI as a head start or use it as something to fight against – it's an amazing time to be a problem solver!

—

I agree with Ali and I rather like this idea of using AI as a way to get a "head start" on the work, getting the more obvious stuff out of the way, and maybe going a bit beyond—so a human can take some big, weird, risky creative swings downstream. It's similar to the way I proposed earlier that AI could be used to replace group brainstorms. It shouldn't replace human creativity—it should make more space for it.

How to influence with influencers.

Back in Chapter 6, I outlined some of the challenges with influencer campaigns, and how an over-reliance on them can turn brands into zombies. Jumping into celebrity or influencer partnerships without first establishing a strong brand—like the Crypto.com Super Bowl spot featuring Matt Damon—is just a waste of money, because the celebrity's brand invariably overwhelms the brand he's promoting. The most effective pairings are grounded in an alignment between an influencer and a brand.

Hopefully, you've found my argument above persuasive—that building brands with celebrity campaigns isn't easy. It requires first and foremost a strong brand foundation and casting based on shared relevance and personality. There's some risk involved. Even after you get those things just right, you have to ensure the celebrity brand remains subservient to the master brand. All those caveats aside, influencer marketing can be an effective instrument in a marketer's toolbox.

I thought it would be useful to speak to someone who knows a lot more about how to craft influencer campaigns than me. So I interviewed Lydia Cox, who you heard from in the last chapter, and who leads Digitas' social media practice.

JL: What are some of the most common mistakes brands make with influencer campaigns?

LC: Inauthenticity. The best brands have an established point of view and find influencers that align with that story. There is a shared value in the collaboration. The worst influencer campaigns are based on inauthentic collaboration and/or simply hawking products. No one believes that Beyonce uses only drugstore makeup or that Kylie Jenner is starting a revolution with a soda.

JL: What are the hallmarks of a successful influencer campaign?

LC: Community engagement! Of course marketers want to look at things like reach or follower growth but the best metric and hallmark of success is engagement. This is rooted in the idea that the best campaigns drive a natural alignment/engagement because they're not just a product shill, they're rooted in a shared value. For example: a makeup brand has full access to NY Fashion Week and gives an up-and-coming influential designer all access. Fun! Shared value for both. Makeup brand gets borrowed clout, fashion designer gets true value from the collaboration. And their fans benefit. So if you're creating a partnership rooted in this idea of shared value, the influencer's communities should come along for the ride and naturally participate, which is much more impactful for the brand than things like reach metrics.

JL: How do you measure the success of an influencer campaign?

LC: It depends on what you want to get out of it but I would look at things like engagement, reach and quality of commentary. Don't forget that social media is a direct line to your consumers and creates a feedback loop of information, so if you're actively listening you can really understand what the community is craving.

There are cases where brands are looking to borrow influence or clout from people in specific communities as a way to break through with their growth targets, in which case I would treat this more like a media play where I'm looking at things like reach. But I would argue that this is a shorter term and transactional view.

JL: What makes a good brief for an influencer campaign? What are the key elements?

LC: Simplicity, clearly defined roles and flattery. Really defining the role of the brand and influencer in the context of the campaign and making it clear what is the brand trying to do and why do they need this particular influencer as the lynchpin. Also, as visual as possible.

JL: When you think about selecting influencers for a campaign—casting if you will—how do you go about that? Is it about reach? Brand relevance? A particular community you're trying to win over?

LC: I find it's the unexpected people who tend to drive the best outcomes. For example, if you're working with a fast food brand, of course the most obvious choice are the "mukbang burger" influencers. But you can get a lot more breakthrough with someone who is all about healthy/happy lifestyle balance, or hungover eats, or trying new things. Going off the beaten path is so so critical to break through.

Looking at influencer selection through a community lens is also critically important because that gives us ability to really grow and build a relationship over time. Communities are defined by shared values and interests and passions so they tend to be flat with little nodes of influential people or topics that send ripples through the community. Finding the people who can create the ripples but having the understanding that you're talking to an interest-aligned group rallied around a passion is how you're going to get the most out of the relationship (essentially a focus group). A brand-first approach is finding story-aligned influencers who have shared values. These are the people who naturally fit in with whatever the brand is trying to do. With a media-first approach, you identify influencers who can reach a particular audience you're trying to grow with. If you can identify these people and then apply a more story-driven lens, it can be a win.

JL: What are the risks associated with investing in influencers and how do you manage them?

LC: I think the biggest risk is creating shitty or cringe content. The other answer to this question is brand safety. The thing about influencers is they've built their entire careers on opening up these personal sides of themselves and letting people into their own personal worlds. We are all made up of many facets and many communities so partnering with a human (rather than a celeb for example where they are much more controlled, have PR people), you do risk aligning with topics you may not have wanted to as a brand.

JL: Are there certain categories you think are particularly suitable for influencers? Why do you think that is?

LC: To me it's about finding shared values - IMHO, the best brands have human-like qualities, where you know how the brand might react to a certain conversation or how they might speak or how they might activate. Finding people aligned to those qualities is key. The worst influencer partnerships are based on things like follower count or reach or media alignment where you get poor quality content that can never break through. You WANT people with strong personal brands who the brand would essentially want to hang out with if they were a real person. Of course this presents risks and monitoring is critical, but when done right it can really deliver impact.

JL: You've had a front-row seat to the evolution of influencer marketing. What's changed? What hasn't?

LC: Disclosures have gotten way more serious - the way we have to work with FTC disclosures while still maintaining a lo-fi and authentic approach is a lot more real. We've seen huge brands get fined for millions because they activate huge campaigns without any real guardrails. Overall these rules are a good thing because there can be so much snake oil sold and people are so incredibly impressionable. More recently, this group of Welsh people who went to NYC just to eat crappy fast food ran into problems with a trip to Vegas where they realized they couldn't actually post the content they were being paid to film because they didn't have work visas. Oopsies.

The scale has also really grown. Influencers are a critical component to social media and arguably the entire marketing mix. I've read the influencer industry overall is worth something like $250B. Wild.

We've also seen a lot of the tried and true tactics stop working and become cringe - it's really really obvious when the partnership is paid and transactional, so there's more pressure to create true story. With the decentering of moderation and safety for many of the social platforms, I wonder if we may see more of a shift back to this wild west of the early days regarding disclosures etc.

JL: What are some noteworthy trends you're seeing in influencer marketing?

LC: Micro influencers, creators and brand advocates. We're seeing so many more brands activate with micro influencers because they can achieve quality content with people on the rise, they can support the up-and-comers and save money. Creators play a similar role and can scratch the itch of lo-fi content which still remains a challenge for most brands.

JL: There's a lot of uncertainty in social media. Facebook has an aging audience. There's a lot of toxicity with Instagram. X is a cesspool. And the future of TikTok is in doubt. How do you think about all this when you look to the future of influencer marketing?

LC: The one thing that has stayed constant in this insane social media landscape is change, so I think as a rag tag group of trauma bonded social people, we are ready for what's next. It's interesting to see the pendulum swing towards platforms like Reddit, YouTube (Shorts in particular) and Pinterest. Happy places for many. I don't see influencers going away and I don't see a de-emphasis on the formats like short form vertical videos. To me, it's the platforms and nuance that will undoubtedly change.

Fireworks over the lighthouse.

Back in Chapter 7, I took aim at what I derisively called "Stuntvertising"—stunts that have little if anything to do with a brand's core offering, but are designed to generate a lot of PR buzz and social media engagement. As I argued, getting attention isn't enough. To remain strong, brands need to consistently attract the right kind of attention for the right reasons.

Here's the good news. When stunts (or activations, if you prefer) are done well, they can amplify the brand in a way traditional paid advertising doesn't. Remember what David Droga said about wanting to move away from setting off fireworks to tending lighthouses? To quote a common Internet meme, I say: "Why not both?" There's no reason why a brand can't set off fireworks above its lighthouse—to get attention in order to remind people what it stands for. But as is the case with all great advertising, that's just harder to do. Let's take a look at three examples of stunts that did more than generate short-term buzz—they helped build brands.

One note: I'm not using the word "stunt" here disparagingly. I think of a stunt as an intentionally publicized, focused action a brand takes at a particular moment in time. The most important distinction between a stunt and a regular advertisement is that in a stunt, a brand has to actually do something, not just say something.

REI: #OptOutside.

REI has been synonymous with the outdoors for decades. Founded in Seattle in 1938 as a modest co-op offering equipment to mountain climbing enthusiasts, it currently operates 190 stores in 43 states, with annual sales approaching $4B per year. Interestingly, one of the reasons REI grew to these heights can be, in part, credited to what we'd call an earned media stunt today. In 1963, Jim Whittaker—the company's first full-time employee and later served as its CEO—became the first American to summit Mount Everest. The expedition was covered extensively by the media, and in 1965, CBS television aired a slickly-produced, highly-rated documentary about it. In the wake of all that free publicity, over the next few years, REI's membership grew 400% and sales topped $1M for the first time. The right stunt can work!

By the 1980s, REI branched out from mountaineering gear and started selling camping, biking and kayaking equipment— all to advance its ethos of "outdoors for everyone." In 2015, building on that, REI starting talking about its belief that "an outdoor life is a life well lived." All that set the stage for the historic stunt the brand pulled off on Black Friday of that year. The origins of Black Friday date to 1939, when America was still recovering from the Great Depression. Retailers complained to President Franklin D. Roosevelt that the Thanksgiving holiday, which had since the Civil War fallen on the last day of November, was too close to Christmas, and urged him to move it back in order to give shoppers an extra weekend to spend money at their establishments before Santa's arrival.

FDR obliged, to the delight of everyone except apparently the town of Plymouth, Massachusetts and college football teams, as the *New York Times* reported.

Roosevelt to Move Thanksgiving; Retailers for It, Plymouth Is Not

Football Schedule Makers Also Get a Headache, With Season Set to End With Fifth Thursday in November

Maybe I've just forgotten, but I don't remember advertisers explicitly mentioning Black Friday in ads when I was growing up in the '80s. But by the late 1990s, it had definitely become a thing. Retailers like Walmart and Macy's started opening their doors earlier to aggressively promote their Black Friday sales. Then something shifted into higher gear in the early 2000s. Retailers introduced Cyber Monday and all of a sudden, Black Friday became a week-long event. And it worked. In 2005, the first year of Cyber Monday, Black Friday sales (including the weekend) were $26B. By 2012, the number had ballooned to a staggering $59B. Black Friday had, in a sense, become an unofficial national holiday in its own right. It had arguably reached the same level of importance to marketers as the Super Bowl or March Madness. It wasn't a question if your brand was going to have a Black Friday promotion, it was a question of how big you were going to go. After all, a retailer would have to be nuts to sit out a week when Americans shelled out nearly $60B. Not capitalizing on it was simply unthinkable. But that's exactly what REI—and their agency Venables Bell & Partners—decided to do.

On October 26, 2015, REI released a video on social channels of CEO Jerry Stritzke announcing they would close their stores on Black Friday and encouraged everyone to spend the day outside. "We'd rather be in the mountains than in the aisles" was a particularly memorable line from the video, which also included the campaign hashtag #OptOutside. People were encouraged to use the hashtag and share photos of what they were doing outside, and a microsite served as a hub for the campaign and featured an interactive tool that helped people discover outdoor activities. On Black Friday, REI's website went dark and reiterated the #OptOutside message. The campaign was also supported by a press release and out-of-home advertising.

The results were nothing short of astonishing. Try these on for size:

- 1.2B social media impressions
- 2.7B media impressions within 24 hours
- 6.7 total media impressions
- 3.6x increase in in-store visits
- 9.3% increase in revenue

– 23% increase in digital sales
– 14% increase in brand awareness

And all this after closing all their stores on the busiest shopping day of the year. Not too shabby.

Those numbers, gaudy as they are, don't quite convey how huge #OptOutside was. It was all over the news for weeks. REI had struck a cultural nerve. Before #OptOutside launched, there was a growing sense that Black Friday was getting a little out of control. It seemed like, every year during Black Friday week, videos of shoppers getting crushed in pre-dawn stampedes at big box stores would make the rounds on social media and on the news. REI said what everyone was thinking out loud: "this has all gotten to be a bit much." As of 2025, REI is still closing on Black Friday, so #OptOutside wasn't just a one-off.

The #OptOutside Black Friday stunt was so successful because it amplified what the brand had already been known for. It was a bold, dramatic action aligned with their mission and their values, and it was planned around a moment in time that was highly relevant to the brand, when everyone was paying attention. It paid off, massively. It shot fireworks over REI's lighthouse.

Whirlpool: Care Counts.

Since they introduced the world's first automatic washing machine in 1948, Whirlpool has been the category's dominant player. By 2024, the brand's market share in the US was a whopping 46%, more than doubling up their next two competitors Samsung (18%) and LG (17%). So odds are, if you stopped 100 random people in Times Square and asked them to name a washing machine brand, most would answer, "Whirlpool."

For decades, the brand hung its hat on products and features with the promise,"make your world a little easier."

But in 2014, with the help of their agency, Digitas, they pivoted to a more purpose-driven brand positioning with the platform, "Every day, care." And that set the stage for the "Care Counts."

Armed with a new purpose, Whirlpool and Digitas started digging around and discovered something both shocking and heartbreaking: large numbers of children across the country were missing school because they were embarrassed about not having clean clothes. Studies showed kids who miss school regularly are seven times more likely to drop out.

Rather than just launch a traditional ad campaign drawing attention to this problem, Whirlpool decided to actually do something about it. They installed washing machines and dryers in 17 at-risk schools in Fairfield, California and St. Louis, Missouri. Partnering with educational experts and data scientists, over the course of a school year, they tracked which students were using the machines and how often. The results were astonishing: 90% of students who participated showed improved attendance, in many cases, up to two weeks.

Whirlpool publicly released the results in May of 2016 in a widely-shared video, and in 2017, expanded "Care Counts" to 60 schools. "Care Counts" won a boatload of accolades for Whirpool and its agencies Digitas and Ketchum (PR), snagging a Grand Prix for Creative Data at the Cannes Lions International Festival of Creativity, Pencils at both D&AD and The One Show, a Gold Clio, an Effie, and on and on. It drove business results as well. In the wake of the activation, the brand had its first year-over-year sales growth in five years. It also produced increases in purchase consideration and household penetration. By 2024, "Care Counts" had become a robust program that had grown to reach 164 schools in 41 states, affecting some 50,000 students.

As was the case with REI's #OptOutside, "Care Counts" amplified what people already knew about the brand and what its product was famous for. And it wasn't a one-off. It became a long-term investment that paid dividends for the brand over the years.

Pedigree: Adoptable

The Pedigree Petfoods brand dates to the 1980s, when its parent company Mars consolidated its dog food products under one brand. In 2008, the company established the Pedigree Foundation, a non-profit dedicated to finding homes for shelter dogs. The foundation is, by itself, an excellent illustration of a brand understanding the importance of purpose and action as a means—not only to balance commercial interests with doing good in the world—but to elevate and augment itself above its products and paid advertising.

The challenge for Pedigree was they could only devote a small portion of their paid media budget to promote their dog adoption efforts. In the wake of the Covid pandemic (2020-2021), there was, sadly, a huge spike in the number of dogs in shelters. But what if Pedigree could turn every one of its ads into a dog adoption ad? That's exactly what they (and their agency, Colenso BBDO) did with "Adoptable."

Using AI—specifically, "a stable diffusion machine-learning model"—they were able to convert photos of dogs snapped by local shelters into glowing, studio-quality portraits, which they could seamlessly integrate into their paid advertising. AI not only made this retouching process possible, it did so a scale that would've been too cost-prohibitive by hand. Using first party data, they matched a shelter dog with a specific location. A QR code linked to that dog's adoption page. These ads appeared in all digital mediums—including digital out-of-home, social, and display.

"Adoptable" produced eye-popping results when it was rolled out in New Zealand:

- 600% increase in adoptions
- 50% of shelter dogs featured were adopted within two weeks
- 6x increase in site visits to dog profiles
- 6x increase in shelter visits
- 4.5x increase in time spent on profile pages

It also won a number of fancy awards, including the brand's first-ever Grand Prix Lion (for Outdoor), as well as cleaning up at the Clios and London International Awards. Pedigree plans on rolling out "Adoptable" in other regions, including North America.

Just like #OptOutside and "Care Counts," "Adoptable" amplified what people already knew about Pedigree. It aligned with their product and their DNA, and brilliantly married their commercial interests to their charitable pursuits.

Compare what REI, Whirpool, and Pedigree did to some of the Zombie Brand stunts I mentioned in Chapter 7: Coors Light installing climate-change fighting roofing, State Street Global Advisors commissioning a bronze statue of a little girl—a cat food brand growing a coral reef. Those fireworks may have generated a great deal of attention, but because they were so far removed from their brand's lighthouse, it was fleeting. But there's no reason why stunts or activations can't build brands, as these three brands and their agencies proved.

Epilogue: Death to Zombie Brands!

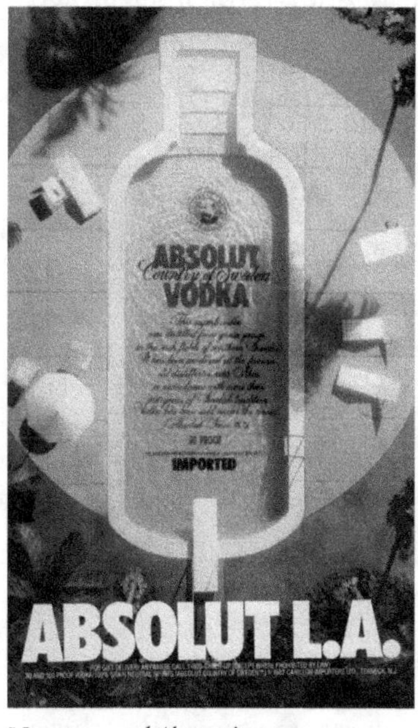

How it started / how it's going.

I hope *Zombie Brands* has done a good job of explaining just how brands went from crafting things that look like the stuff on the left to churning out the disposable junk on the right, what the implications are of that—and what can be done about it. Here's a brief summary of the argument I've laid out in the book.

(1) Technology—specifically the Internet, digital media, the smartphone and social media—have gradually degraded

brands' distinctiveness and humanity. Stunts, influencers, and "shiny object syndrome"—coinciding with marketers' broad shift from persuasion to targeting—eroded them even further.

(2) The predominant media in the smartphone-centric ecosystem are not ideal formats for delivering emotional connections with audiences. Emotional impact is what makes advertising more effective and creates long-term brand growth.

(3) The current media landscape as it stands in 2026 is unstable and growing more so. The four major social platforms are all undergoing some sort of transformation, their user experience is degrading, and smartphones are increasingly viewed as addictive and harmful.

(4) Brands can reverse the ill-effects of these trends, regain their appeal, and win over the youngest generations using a blend of new technologies such as AI to go with more traditional media that is often overlooked—as well as a more brand-centric, strategic approach to the use of influencers and stunts.

OK, you might think, that all makes some sense. But this all feels like a lot of work. Do marketers really have to go through all that trouble? Aren't brands doing pretty well as it is? Those are fair questions in a time of shrinking budgets, timelines, and CMO tenures. But I think there are three reasons to believe simply staying the course is a mistake.

The first is lurking there in that third point—the instability of the current media landscape, anchored by the smartphone. I don't think it's going to vanish tomorrow or next year, but it is clearly showing signs of strain and it's inevitable that it will eventually be disrupted. As I discussed in Chapter 8, one thing we should've learned over the past half century is that media habits can and will change—often very quickly. By some estimates, in 2025, Americans are spending just over five hours per day on their smartphones, which is pretty close to the number of hours people were watching broadcast television in 1980. And then, well, this happened.

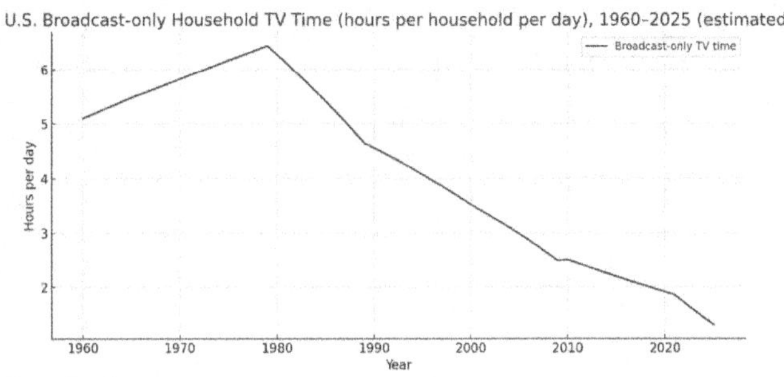

Made with ChatGPT

I seriously doubt there were many advertising and marketing professionals in 1980 saying, "Well, we've officially hit peak-broadcast TV. It's all downhill from here!" They had every reason to believe the number would continue to rise or at least hold. Same goes for other forms of media. People read newspapers and magazines, until they didn't. Brands that do the hard work now of sharply defining themselves, building emotional connections through impactful creative and regularly showing up in high-attention media will be best able to make the transition to whatever comes next. Brands that don't will be left behind.

The second reason I think the current path brands are on is unsustainable is we've reached a critical tipping point.

Take a look at these two slides from Effie and System1's 2025 report titled, "The Creative Dividend: How creativity multiplies profit."

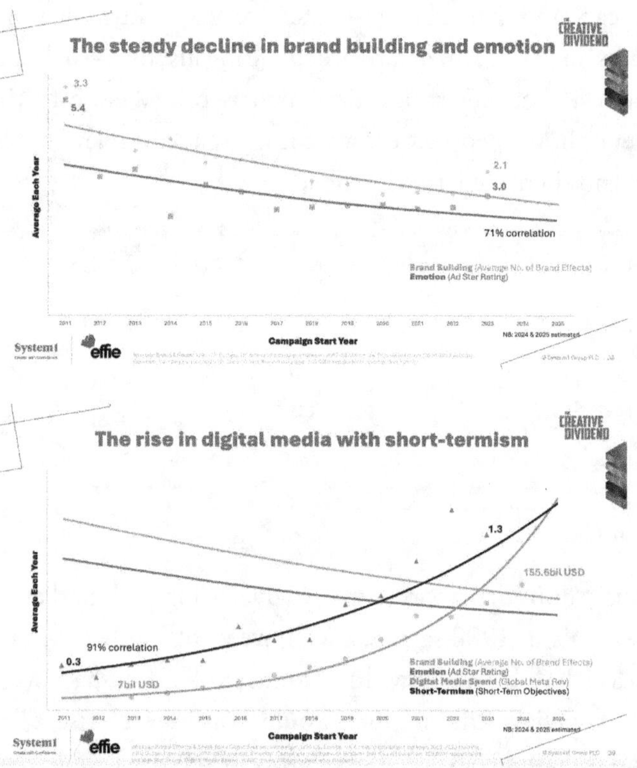

Over the past fifteen years—the Zombie Brand era—brands have been steadily decreasing their investments in long-term, emotional brand building advertising while increasing their spend on "short-termism"—campaigns and ads deployed for short-term results—which coincides with digital media spend. Somewhere around 2022-2024, short-termism overtook brand-building campaigns for the first time. Want to guess what's going to happen next? Just ask Adidas and Nike. Time and time again, we've seen that, when brands neglect brand-building for too long, they invariably decline.

Third, and probably the most important reason brands need to change, is people really hate Zombie Brands. The ad industry is supposed to be more data-driven these days, but it keeps ignoring all the data that shows this. Just take a look at these headlines of articles over the past six years, based on surveys and polls.

"The Advertising Industry Has a Problem: People Hate Ads," —*New York Times,* 2019.

"Most consumers are creeped out by ads that follow them across devices"—*eMarketer/Insider Intelligence,* 2021.

"Has advertising lost its connection with consumers?"— YouGov, 2022.

"70% of consumers find ads annoying, new survey finds" —*MediaCat,* 2023.

"Everyone hates annoying digital ads" —*Fast Company*, 2024.

"Most American Adults Are Creeped Out by Personalized Ads" —MarketingCharts, based on a YouGov Survey, 2025

These headlines should be blaring, red-alert warnings for marketers that something is seriously wrong with advertising. They look even more dire when you consider the youngest generations—Gen-Z and Gen-Alpha—have grown up during the Zombie Brand era. The vast majority of the ads they've seen over the course of their entire lives look like that pathetic Absolut banner. That has huge implications over the next two decades, when they reach the prime spending ages of adulthood.

I think about this a lot. By the time I went off to college, I had very strong brand preferences across dozens of categories—several that I hadn't even aged into yet. Just to name a few, jeans (Levi's), sunglasses (Ray-Ban), clothing store (GAP), cars (Jeep, Porsche), computers (Apple), sneakers (Nike), toothpaste (Aquafresh), watches (Timex), toothbrushes (Reach), vodka (Absolut), dress shirts (Polo by Ralph Lauren), electric razors (Braun), fast food (McDonald's), TVs and stereos (Sony), ice cream (Ben & Jerry's), and I could go on. I'm still loyal to many of these. I formed those attachments in large part because of those brands' consistent investment in crafting high-impact, high-attention advertising when I was growing up in the 1980s and 1990s. Some of the ads I saw, read, or heard were superb, some were just okay, some were annoying. But they kept showing up, month after month, and year after year, and many won me over.

But if I asked my sons, who were born in 2005 and 2007, to name their favorite clothing store or brand of jeans or sunglasses, they would just stare at me and blink. They simply don't have preferences for any of this stuff, and they don't share my attachments to any of the brands above, including my life-long loyalty to Apple.

For a Gen-Xer like me, Apple is the IIe, the two Steves, "1984", the original Macintosh, "the computer for the rest of us," the Lisa, "Think Different," the iPod, "1,000 Songs in Your Pocket," U2's "Vertigo", "Mac vs. PC," the "Tangerine" iMac, the PowerBook, the Yao Ming/Mini-Me spot, "Shot on an iPhone"—and so on. But to my sons, Apple is literally just the iPhone—a commodity, the default choice, frustratingly limited by a corporate-controlled, closed ecosystem. To them, Apple is "mid."

So here's the trillion-dollar question. How will Apple win them—and others their age like them—over? I'm actually not sure if they can—that ship might have already sailed. But I do know that social posts, banners and emails alone aren't going to cut it. Not by a long shot. Now imagine that same scenario playing out across all the categories I've listed above.

The brands that see this as an opportunity will be rewarded. Take Liquid Death. In 2019, the year the company started selling its canned water with its punk rock name and sensibility, no one–I mean no one–was asking for another water brand. The market was already ridiculously oversaturated. But in a few short years, Liquid Death has grown into a $1.4B beverage company. How? By doing many of the things I've covered in the past several chapters. Bold logo in a custom typeface? Check. Distinctive packaging? Check. An original and engaging brand voice? Check. A constant stream of hilariously entertaining long-form videos? Check. How about a heavy metal album on Spotify with song titles and lyrics based on negative product reviews? Check, check, check.

But in the Zombie Brand era, many brands have been coasting on the equity they'd built up through decades and decades of investment. Now the bill's due. To be prepared for the inevitable disruption that's coming to the current media landscape and connect with the next generations, brands will have to stop acting like zombies. They'll have to stop relying so heavily on postcards, and get back to playing the long game, investing in the slow, hard, steady work of tending to their lighthouses. They'll have to make people think, laugh, cry, and desire them.

They'll have to be human again.

www.ingramcontent.com/pod-product-compliance
Lightning Source LLC
Chambersburg PA
CBHW071510140726
47997CB00005B/1923